MACHIAVELLI'S
THE PRINCE

MACHIAVELLI'S

The Prince

An Elizabethan Translation

EDITED *with an introduction*
and notes from a manuscript
in the collection of
Mr. JULES FURTHMAN

By HARDIN CRAIG

CHAPEL HILL *The University*
OF NORTH CAROLINA PRESS

PREFATORY NOTE

Books and articles about Machiavelli's *Il Principe* are extremely numerous. In the following edition of an Elizabethan translation of that work into English we have attempted to restrict our reference to those works in Machiavellian scholarship which bear on the task in hand, and to those only. A bibliography of Machiavelli will be found in the *Cambridge Modern History*, Chapter VI, "The Renaissance." Pasquale Villari, *Niccolò Machiavelli e i suoi tempi*, third edition (Firenze, 1913-1914), of which work there is an English translation, is a mine of information, bibliographical and otherwise. In the task of editing the present text there was naturally much use of Adolph Gerber, *Niccolò Machiavelli: Die Handschriften, Ausgaben und Übersetzungen seiner Werke im 16. und 17. Jahrhundert* (3 vols., Gotha, München, 1912-1913). *Il Principe di Niccolò Machiavelli*, Testo critico con introduzione e note a cura di Giuseppe Lisio (Firenze, 1899) is important for its study of the text of *Il Principe*. The centenary edition by Guido Mazzoni (Roma, 1927) serves somewhat the same purpose. The text of this edition has been superseded by the edition of Mazzoni and Casella (1928). A more complete bibliography, of a general nature, is given by Norsa in *Il principio della forsa nel pensiero politico di Machiavelli* (1936). Signore Lisio's general edition of *Il Principe* (Firenze, 1900) is most useful for matters of history and interpretation. The edition of *Il Principe* by Russo is also valuable. The best English edition is that of L. Arthur Burd (Oxford, 1891), for which Lord Acton wrote a learned and admirable introduction. F. Meinecke's introduction to *Der Fürst und kleinere Schriften* (1923) should also be mentioned. For Machiavelli in England, a well worked subject, one should consult the still valuable *Machiavelli and the Elizabethan Drama* by Edward Meyer (Weimar, 1897) and the more recent *Machiavelli and the Elizabethans* by Mario Praz (1928). Piero Rébora, *Il "Machiavellismo" nel dramma elisabettiano* (Milan, 1925) and Wyndham Lewis, *The Lion and the Fox* (London, 1927) should also be mentioned. Hans Beck, *Machiavelismus in der englischen Renaissance* (Duisberg, 1935), reviews the subject carefully and makes minor contributions to it. An unpublished thesis for the M.A. degree (1935) by Jeannette Fellheimer in the library of the University of London, "The Englishman's Conception of the Italian in the Age of Shakespeare," presents in Chapter IV, "The Elizabethan Attitude to Machiavelli," an excellent study of Machiavelli and the Elizabethans. The author has examined the State Papers, the publications of the Historical Manuscripts Commission, and various other new sources of information. She has also reexamined the works of authors known to have referred to Machiavelli and has made studies of Bacon's and of Ralegh's relation to him. She lists without comment the four Harley manuscripts which are discussed in the following introduction. Among the most valuable works on Machiavelli are those of Allan H. Gilbert. *Machiavelli's Prince and its Fore-runners* (Durham, N. C., 1938) is a study of *The Prince* as a typical *de Regimine Principum* and a work of great erudition, which contains an excellent bibliography. *Machiavelli: The Prince and other Works* (Chicago, 1941) is a carefully indexed introduction to the political thought of the great Florentine.

The only description of manuscripts used in this edition is that contained in Professor Napoleone Orsini's *Studii sul Rinascimento italiano in Inghilterra* (Firenze, 1937), pp. 1-19. The same material in briefer form is presented in "Elizabethan Manuscript Translations of Machiavelli's *Prince*," *Journal of the Warburg Institute* (I, 166-69). Professor Orsini describes in detail the four Harley manuscript translations of *The Prince* and also that in Bodleian MS Ashmole 792.3. Since he did not have the use of the Furthman manuscript, his conjectural arrangement of the versions of group A differs slightly from that in the following pages. The reader is referred to Professor Orsini's study for various details. His book above mentioned and his *Bacone e Machiavelli* (Genova, 1936) offer distinguished treatments of Machiavelli in England. It was through the great kindness of Professor Orsini that the editor was able to locate a seventh manuscript of *The Prince* at Queen's College, Oxford— Queen's College MS No. 251.

In the following edition of *The Prince* of Machiavelli, the Furthman manuscript has been used as a basis. The collations (given in the notes) of this manuscript with other manuscripts of the same version are complete only as regards the relations of the Furthman manuscript. Only such variants have been recorded as are necessary to establish the text and to reproduce, as far as possible, the original anonymous translation of which the various manuscripts considered in the introduction and notes are more or less perfect reproductions. Variations in spelling, punctuation, and grammatical construction have been disregarded unless they bear on the question of text. Casual blunders, of which there are many in Harley 6795, have not been recorded. Specifically, since Harley 967 follows the Furthman manuscript closely, not all agreements have been listed. These two manuscripts may be assumed to agree unless differences are noted. The object has been to publish a correct Elizabethan version of the great Renaissance classic and to preserve the interesting scribal characteristics (spelling, punctuation, capitalization, italicization) of the Furthman manuscript. The result is a free-running, bold piece of Elizabethan English, somewhat euphuistic, always intelligent and vivacious, in a form characteristic of the practice of the best writers of the late sixteenth century. One would like to know the name of the translator and, particularly, the names of the persons who, apparently in considerable numbers, read his work; but both the translator and his readers probably lived freer from molestation by leaving the world in ignorance of these things.

Certain matters with reference to the history of the manuscript and to the hand in which it is written have been worked out by Mr. Furthman. He has turned these over to the editor and has been most generous in supplying photographs of manuscripts for the editor's use.

There are in the Furthman manuscript a considerable number of marginal comments, mainly moral reflections and references to books. They are in a seventeenth-century hand probably belonging to the second quarter of the century. These annotations are recorded in the notes, where some indications of the date of the writing will be found.

CONTENTS

INTRODUCTION

INTRODUCTION

MACHIAVELLI's *Il Principe* was very popular for a score of years after its publication. The pope authorized its issue on August 23, 1531; there were two editions in 1532 and twenty-five within the next twenty years. But the tide turned. Cardinal Pole asserted in his *Apologia* (ed. Brixiae, 1744, I, 152) that the works of Machiavelli had been written by the hand of Satan himself. Magio denounced Machiavelli to the Inquisition in 1550. Ambrogio Caterino attacked him violently in *De Libris a Christiano detestandi* in 1552, and in that year Machiavelli was assaulted by the great Portuguese orator Ossorio in *De Nobilitate Christiana*. Other attacks were to follow. Paulus Jovius (*Eclog.* cap. 87) in 1557 declared Machiavelli an atheist. It is said also [1] that the Jesuits, as whose partner in iniquity the later years of the sixteenth century chose to regard Machiavelli, burned him in effigy at Ingolstadt. The Jesuit attack, which was by far the most serious of all, was led by Antonio Possevino (*De N. Machiavelli ... quibusdam Scriptis*, 1592). Finally, the Inquisition

[1] See Villari (1892), II, 263.

in an edict published in 1559 decreed the utter destruction of Machiavelli's works, and the Council of Trent confirmed the edict in 1564.

It was urged against the Florentine that in the *Discorsi*, II, 2 he had made an offensive comparison between Christianity and Paganism and that in *Il Principe* (chapter vi) he had treated Moses as a mere statesman of history. Back of these special charges lay Machiavelli's rejection of papal infallibility. The attack came from the Catholics, but was by no means confined to them, and its grounds were well taken. We may also believe that the temper of the times had undergone such changes that Machiavelli's pagan frankness was no longer widely acceptable and that his political "realism" was shocking to the later age. The story of Gentillet's *Discours sur les Moyens de bien gouverner et maintenir en bonne paix un Royaume ... contre Nicolas Machiavel, Florentin* (Paris, 1576), with its slanderous misrepresentation of Machiavelli, and of Simon Patericke's translation of that work into English, is well known. With Gentillet's libel and all that had gone before it, Machiavelli's reputation suffered a blackening from which it has never completely recovered. To the Elizabethan world in general Machiavelli was an atheist, and it could not have been safe to be associated with him. But he was a very great writer and thinker, and the evidence that English translations of *The Prince* were circulating, perhaps secretly, during the reign of Queen Elizabeth indicates, not that men were turning to atheism (there is nothing in *The Prince* to feed atheism), but that the true value of Machiavelli's work was finding recognition at least among certain groups of readers. Machiavelli did not lose and has never lost his hold upon the class of persons whom he addressed, namely princes and rulers of states.

There was nothing about Machiavelli's *Il Principe* that

would endear it to the Protestants except its rough treatment of the popes Alexander VI and Julius II and except also its denunciation by the Jesuits, but it seems to have been from a Protestant source that a new reputation for Machiavelli, that of a political controversialist, took its rise. Pietro Perna, an Italian Protestant born at Lucca and long an important printer at Basle, issued a Latin translation of *Il Principe* in 1560. The translator was Sylvester Telius or Tegli of Foligno, about whom very little is known. The title-page of this work is as follows: *Nicolai Machiavelli Reip. Florentinæ a secretis, ad Laurentium Medicem de Principe libellus: nostro quidem seculo apprimè vtilis & necessarius, non modo ad principatum adipiscendum, sed & regendum & conseruandum: nunc primum ex Italico in Latinum sermonem versus per Syluestrum Telium Fulginatum.* Basiliæ apud Petrum Pernam. M.D.LX. This Latin translation was later associated with a group of controversial works.

Telius, who translated the work into Latin, replaced Machiavelli's introductory epistle dedicating the work to Lorenzo de' Medici with a dedication of his own to a Polish knight, Abraham Sbaski, and none of the subsequent editions of the Latin version seems to have included Machiavelli's epistle. Telius says in the complimentary language of the time that he has undertaken the work of translation of his own accord, that he has sought to supply a general need by rendering the work available in the Latin language, and that Sbaski is a fit and proper person to appreciate the work. Since the departure of Sbaski from Geneva, Telius has lived in the household of the generous Nicolaus Liena, jurisconsult of Lucca. Liena has told him of the extraordinary qualities of Sbaski, and Paulus Arnulfinus and Nicolaus Gallus have confirmed the report. These testimonies and his own limited acquaintance with Sbaski have caused him to offer his work to the favor of the Polish knight. Telius himself has suffered much from the slanders of the times, and this too has made him rejoice at finding a man so upright, so cultured, and so religious as Sbaski. Therefore he presents this little spark of his genius, hoping that he may not seem to flatter but that his sincerity may be recognized. He is not ignorant of the fact that many authors have declared it a crime to read Machiavelli on the ground that the minds of men may thereby be led astray from religious truth. On the other hand, many have praised Machiavelli and recognized his genius. There is no greater reason to condemn Machiavelli than to condemn such secular authors as Martial, Ovid, Lucian, and others. Indeed, we know that Justin, Clement, and other holy men were acquainted with profane authors and used them for the support of true doctrine. The knowledge of evil is not evil. Evil is of the mind itself. The epistle is dated Basiliæ XIII. Calend. Aprilis. M.D.LX.

The translation is a very good one. There are a few condensations in the text and some omissions or expurgations. For example, Telius omits from the first paragraph of chapter xviii the statement that one sees in the light of the times that the most successful princes have been compelled to disregard fidelity to their plighted troth and honesty in their dealings. There are a few other changes of the same sort. Italian names in the original have been translated into Latin, so that we have Flaminia for Romagna, Mediolanum for Milano, Traiani Portus for Piombino, Gallia Cisalpina for Lombardy, etc. As before said, the dedicatory letter of Machiavelli to Lorenzo de' Medici is wanting in all editions of the Latin version.

The Bibliothèque Nationale catalogues a copy of this translation as published by Perna at Basle in 1570, which, though it has not been consulted directly, seems to be a copy of the edition of 1560. It is, however, with an edition of 1580 that the popularity and wide circulation of the Latin translation of *Il Principe* seems to have begun. In this year there was issued by Perna, *Nicolai Machiavelli Princeps, ex Sylvestri Telii Fulginatis traductione diligenter emendata. Adiecta sunt eiusdam argumenti aliorum quorundam contra Machiavellum scripta de potestate & officio Principum, et contra tyrannos*. Basiliæ. Ex officina Petri Perna. M.D.XXC. One issue has an epistle *Typographus candido lectore*. Two other issues of the same year have dedications by Ioan. Nicolaus Stupanus, *medicus et philosophus*, to Christophorus Blauuerus, bishop of Basle. A. Gerber in his *Niccolò Machiavelli* gives an extended account of the issues, legal and otherwise, reflected in these dedications. Besides Tegli's translation of *Il Principe*, the book published in 1580 contains the orations to Augustus *Contra Monarchia* by Agrippa and *Pro Monarchia* by Mecœnas, both from the fifty-second book of the *Historia Romana* of Dion Cassius. Then follows, with separate title-page and separate pagination, the *Vindiciæ contra Tyrannos*.

The book was to go through many editions. The next, with similar title-page and identical contents, is that of 1589. It has neither place nor printer, but the catalogue of the British Museum offers the apparently sound conjecture that the book was printed at Basle. Then followed two similar editions, also without place or publisher, of 1595 and 1599, determined by Gerber to have been published at Hanover by Gulielmus Antonius. A book of the same contents was published in 1599 at Montbéliard (Montisbelgardi) by Foillet (again on the authority of Gerber). The next edition, published in 1600 at Ursel, adds to the collection the *Judicium de Nicolai Machiavelli et Ioannis Bodini quibusdam scriptis* by the Jesuit Antonio Possevino. In this expanded form the book went through two editions at Frankfurt, in 1608 and 1622, and two at Lyons, in 1643 and 1648. The collection is perhaps to be regarded as anti-Machiavellian, but not completely so, and *Il Principe* is at least in learned company.

Meantime there had been at least three translations of *Il Principe* into French, beginning with the excellent version of Guillaume Cappel (Paris, C. Estienne, 1553). There was a translation by Gaspard d'Auvergne (Poitiers, E. de Marnef) in 1563, listed as 1553 by Gerber; reissued in 1586 (Rouen) and in 1613; and in 1571 a translation (really a reworking of Cappel) by the illustrious and prolific Jacques Gohorry: *Le Prince de Nicolas Machiavel secretaire et citoyen florentin. . . . Traduit d'Italien en François auec la vie de l'auteur mesme, par Iaq. Gohory Parisien* (Paris, Robert le Mangnier).

There were thus abundant translations of *Il Principe* into Latin and French during the sixteenth century, but until recently no English translation has been known. It has been supposed that Englishmen, many of whom show familiarity with Machiavelli, knew him only through Gentillet's *Contre-Machiavel*, or through the Italian, the French, or the Latin. There is evidence indeed of a demand for the original in the venture of John Wolfe, a printer who seems to have specialized in the publication of Italian books. Wolfe printed in London *Il Prencipe di Nicolo Machiavelli, al Magnifico Lorenzo di Piero de Medici. Con alcune altre operette, i titoli delle quali trouerai nella seguente facciata,* and also *l Discorsi di Nicolo Machiavelli, sopra la prima Deca di Tito Livio,* with the statement at the foot of each title-page: In Palermo. Appresso gli heredi d'Antoniello degli Antonielli a xxviij. di Gennaio, 1584. It is usually supposed that Wolfe could not have procured a license to publish the works of Machiavelli in England and so resorted to this form of piracy. The *alcune altre operette* referred to on the title-page of *Il Prencipe* are *La vita di Castruccio Castracani, Il modo tenuto dal Duca Valentino nell' amazzare Vitellozzo Vitelli, Oliuerotto da Fermo, il Signor Paolo, & il Duca di Grauina*, together with other minor pieces—the same group, in other words, which has long been associated with *Il Principe*. One might expect that an English translation of *Il Principe* would also include these works, but such is not the case with the translation we are considering. Nobody doubts that the interest in England in Machiavelli, an author widely condemned, was yet sufficiently keen and that the knowledge of his most striking work was widespread.

There is another evidence of English interest in *The Prince* in the existence in manuscript of three translations into English, two of the sixteenth century and the other probably of the early seventeenth. They are herein referred to as A, B, and C. The interrelations of the various manuscripts in which these translations are preserved indicate that one of the versions (A) at least must have been in circulation in considerable numbers. None of the versions just referred to has any ascertainable connection with the first translation that got into print: *Nicholas Machiavel's Prince, also the Life of Castruccio Castracani of Lucca. And the meanes Duke Valentine us'd to put to death Vitelozzo Vitelli, Oliverotto of Fermo, Paul, and the Duke of Gravina.* Translated out of the Italian by E[dward] D[acres]. London, R. Bishop for W. Hils, 1640. (Issued in the Tudor Translations in 1892 and again with an introduction by W. E. C. Baynes at London in 1929.)

The best of the manuscripts of *The Prince* in version A is the folio in the collection of Mr. Jules Furthman of Los Angeles. It is the work of an intelligent copyist. Its orthography and punctuation are so consistent and so much in line with the best practice of the late sixteenth century that they have been carefully preserved in the following text. The manuscript is a brilliant piece of penmanship—the text in a strong, rapid, somewhat conventional secretary hand, and the chapter headings, proper names, verse quotations and aphorisms, in a beautiful Italian hand. The punctuation is light and what has been called rhetorical, that is, used for purposes of guidance and emphasis in reading rather than for grammatical separation and analysis. The Furthman manuscript (hereafter usually referred to as MS) is perhaps not the oldest of those in existence, but it is in the best tradition. Certainly neither it nor any one of those preserved is the original. This manuscript, before it came into the possession of Mr. Furthman, was mentioned in a note in *Giornale storico*, CIV (1934), 177-78. It is there conjectured on rather slight grounds that the translation may be the work of Thomas Bedingfield.

The manuscript of next greatest importance in group A is British Museum, Harley 6795, a folio manuscript of 59 leaves. It lacks folios 45 and 46, but is otherwise complete. It shows both wear and damage. The hand is a competent English secretary without Italian intrusion. The writing has a suggestion of greater age than that of MS, and this suggestion is borne out by the fact that the language is rather more archaic than that of any other manuscript. Professor Orsini (*Studii sul Rinascimento italiano in Inghilterra*, p. 18) notes that the paper used in Harley 6795 was in current use from 1583 to 1597. It is obviously a copy. It leaves out a good many single lines, does not fill the pages with any regularity, and writes the bit of verse with which *The Prince* closes as prose. Now and then, as will be seen by a consultation of the notes, Harley 6795 goes completely wrong as regards the meaning of what is being copied. For example, on page 107, line 1 it turns the reading of MS, *bylde anie certeintie*, into *blind any certen eie*. Nevertheless it supplies the correct text in many places where MS is wanting or in error. This manuscript translation of *The Prince* is bound up with an unrelated miscellaneous group of sixteenth- and mainly seventeenth-century collections and translations from different books—a part of Justus Lipsius, *De Magistratibus*, Cicero, *De Senectute*, and others.

A manuscript translation of *The Prince* (also Group A) which proves to be closely related to Harley 6795, but is certainly not based directly upon it, is Ashmole 792.3 at the Bodleian Library at Oxford. This is also a folio manuscript and also part of a miscellaneous collection bound up in the same volume. It is described in Black's *Catalogue* of the Ashmolean Manuscripts as a fair copy of the time of James I, and this is no doubt correct enough, although the handwriting seems still to be in the established form of Elizabethan secretary. The manuscript of *The Prince* is obviously the oldest in the collection both in handwriting and paper. Ashmole 792 is a rather pretty manuscript, with green rulings, red catchwords, page numbers and running-heads, with occasional use also of red or green ink for ornament or emphasis. This manuscript omits a large part of the third chapter of *The Prince*—the part dealing with Italian politics —and, since the join is complete and the omitted passage a unit, the omission is probably intentional. Ashmole 792 is almost without paragraphing and uses little italic. It is carefully punctuated in a more modern system than that of either MS or Harley 6795. The parallels and variants worked out in the notes to this volume show that Ashmole 792 usually, but not always, agrees in variant readings with Harley 6795. It cannot be the immediate source of that manuscript because of the omission above referred to and because of many cases, some of them essential, in which it agrees with MS in manifestly erroneous readings against Harley 6795. There are so many cases in which Ashmole 792 alone has correct readings that one must believe that it is based upon the original.

In this series (A) there is a fourth manuscript of great interest, Harley 967. It is a quarto, written in a crabbed Elizabethan hand and containing in the same volume no other work than *The Prince*, except a few pages in the hand of the scribe at the end of the translation. Harley 967 agrees so closely with MS that one is safe in saying that Harley 967 is derived immediately from the Furthman manuscript. It follows MS in italicization, paragraphing, and general style, and those cases in which it is found in agreement with Harley 6795 or Ashmole 792 and not with MS as regards the true text, or as regards community of error, are so few and unimportant that they may be fairly attributed to intelligent scribal correction or to accident.

After finishing the copy of the translation, the writer of Harley 967 goes on for a few pages with a rough transcript of the first sixteen paragraphs of *The Copie of a Leter, wrytten by a Master of Arte of Cambridge to his Friend in London, concerning some talke past of late between two worshipful and graue men, about the present state, and some proceedinges of the Erle of Leycester and his friendes in England.* Anno M.D.LXXXIII. This is the famous tractate known as *Leicester's Commonwealth*, reprinted in 1641 and many times since, and the part copied in Harley 967 is a sort of introduction or exordium to that book. The identification of the addendum to Harley 967 with the opening paragraphs of *Leicester's Commonwealth* was made by Professor Orsini in "Elizabethan Manuscript Translations of Machiavelli's *Prince*." (*Loc. cit.*, p. 168 n.)

The Copie of a Leter was printed certainly on the Continent, probably at Antwerp, and is in part a reply to Lord Burghley's *The Execution of Justice in England*, which had been published in 1583 as a defense of the government for having put to death certain Catholics on charges of treason. Burghley's tract is referred to as "a litle boke, then newlie set forth." The execution of Campion, Sherwin, and Briant had taken place on December 1, 1581, and in 1582 Cardinal Allen published anonymously *A Briefe History of the Martyrdom of XII Reverend Priestes, executed within these twelvemonthes for confession and defence of Catholike Faith, but under false Pretence of Treason, a Note of sundrie Things that befel them in their Life and Imprisonment, and a Preface declaring them Innocent.* Latin and Italian [2] translations of this work appeared immediately, and it was in reply to Cardinal Allen that Lord Burghley wrote *The Execution of Justice in England.*

The Copie of a Leter was translated into French and Latin in 1585. It is primarily a libel against the Earl of Leicester, whom it accuses of many crimes. On June 20, 1585 the Queen in Council denounced the work as a slander, and a careful watch seems to have been kept for the book at various ports. Many copies were no doubt seized and destroyed.[3] Copies of the pamphlet grew scarce, and many manuscript transcriptions came into existence. The excerpt made by the

---

[2] Professor Orsini (*Studii sul Rinascimento italiano in Inghilterra,* pp. 8-9, 16-19) offers the suggestion that Petruccio Ubaldini may have seen Wolfe's edition of *Il Principe* through the press and may be responsible for the translation into Italian of Burghley's *The Execution of Justice in England,* since that translation (*Atto della iustitia d'Inghilterra*) was published by Wolfe in 1584. Professor Orsini also suggests that Ubaldini or some of his associates may have made the translation of *Il Principe* into English.

[3] See *History of Queen Elizabeth, Amy Robsart and the Earl of Leicester, being a reprint of Leycesters Commonwealth".* Edited by Frank J. Burgoyne. London, 1904; also article on Leicester in *D.N.B.*

copyist of Harley 967 would probably not have been made before 1585 unless, as is possible, the exordium antedates the printing of *The Copie of a Leter*. The selection in Harley 967 does not follow the printed copy closely, but in one case supplies a reading omitted from the printed text. There is no doubt that *The Copie of a Leter* is given a tone favorable to the Catholics by its chief speaker, a lawyer who is described as a "Temperat Papist." The selections in Harley 967, which contain no allusion to Leicester, are made in such a way as to accentuate this Catholic bias. A short poem which follows the tractate in Harley 967 is openly Catholic in substance. Both of these pieces, of course, condemn Machiavelli. The tractate has, however, a heading which seems to denounce what is to follow as diabolical insinuation in favor of the Papists. At least that seems to be the only reasonable interpretation of *The entrance into the adoration of moloch: (the image state) of own* (?) *making, &c. setled by the artes of Machiauel*. Since Harley 967 rests immediately on the Furthman manuscript, these considerations enable us to form an idea of the date of the latter document. Of course we cannot be sure that the man who was copying the translation of *The Prince* in Harley 967 from another manuscript was not also copying the discursus on Catholic persecution from the same document; but, since the hand in which Harley 967 is written is obviously an Elizabethan hand—and on this point we have the opinion of the authorities on English manuscripts at the British Museum—there is at least a presumption in favor of the dating of Harley 967 in 1585. It is to be remembered that the writer of Harley 967 was copying from the Furthman manuscript. A few leaves have been torn from the end of that manuscript, which just possibly once contained the little discourse.

There are, besides the four already described, three other

manuscripts of *The Prince* in English. Bernard's *Catalogi Librorum Manuscriptorum Angliae et Hiberniae* (Oxford, 1697) lists still another among the manuscripts at York Cathedral, but that seems long ago to have disappeared.

Harley 364 at the British Museum, a folio of miscellaneous contents, contains an English translation of *The Prince* (group B) almost but not quite independent of version A (already described) and apparently completely independent of the Dacres version of 1640. The first twenty-five chapters of *The Prince* in Harley 364 seem to be directly from the Italian and have no connection with version A. The hand is again pronounced to be unquestionably Elizabethan, and the manuscript up to the end of folio 103v seems to be an original, since it has undergone many corrections and changes in the hand of the writer. At the end of folio 103v, in the midst of chapter xxv, the hand changes, and what seems to be the same version goes on in the new hand to the end of chapter xxv. At that point, the beginning of chapter xxvi, *An Exhortation to deliver Italy from the Barbarians*, version A begins. Chapter xxvi and the epistle dedicatory to Lorenzo de' Medici present the same version as the Furthman manuscript, Harley 6795, Ashmole 792, and Harley 967. The parts under consideration seem to agree with the Furthman manuscript rather than with Harley 967, its descendant, or with either of the others, but the variants are not so significant that we can say definitely that these parts of Harley 364 were certainly copied from one or the other of the extant complete manuscripts.

Harley 2292 is a fairly accurate copy of the translation of *The Prince* in Harley 364; that is, it follows the independent translation from the Italian for the first twenty-five chapters and reproduces version A of chapter xxvi and of the epistle dedicatory. Harley 2292, which is a quarto and contains only the translation of *The Prince*, is written in a fine-lined, rather exquisite hand and bears on the title-page the date 3 Augusti, 1724. The writing and spelling are slightly archaic. The manuscript reproduces from Harley 364, where it is signed a:p:k, the following couplet:

> Welcome to me, in measure, and in meane
> too much is naught, yet doe not leave me cleane.

A third translation (C), apparently from the Italian and completely independent of version A, version B, and the Dacres translation of 1640, is to be found in MS No. 251, Queen's College, Oxford. It is a paper manuscript in quarto of 96 leaves, without title, attribution of authorship, or any markings by which it might be identified. H. O. Coxe, *Catalogus Codicum MSS. qui in Collegiis Aulisque Oxoniensibus hodie adservantur* (Oxon., 1852), did not recognize the treatise as *The Prince* and described it as "An essay on the different forms of government, and on the duties of princes, illustrated from the lives and characters of the Roman emperors down to Maximinus." The translation lacks the dedicatory letter of Machiavelli to Lorenzo de' Medici and has no chapter headings or table of contents. It is complete except for about 170 words at the end of the last chapter. Chapter xxiv appears in two versions. The manuscript, which shows little evidence of use, is neatly written in a seventeenth-century hand, probably early. There would be less reason for the making of such a manuscript after the publication of Dacres' translation.

Our interest of course is in version A, and when we inquire into the source of that version, we encounter certain difficulties and perplexities. It is obvious that the unknown translator had before him the Latin version of *Il Principe* as translated by Sylvester Telius. Version A reproduces again and again the phraseology of the Latin text. For example, at the beginning of the third chapter the Italian text reads, *Ma nel principato nuovo consistono le difficultà. E prima, se non è tutto nuovo, ma come membro, che si può chiamare tutto insieme quasi misto. . . .* The Latin renders this, *Sed in eo qui recens principatu, difficultates continentur, tum maximé, si veluti pars adiuncta (ut sic in universum mixtus dici possit) non penitus est novus.* Our version clearly follows the Latin: *But in a newe principality there are som combers, specially yf (as a parte adioyned) it be not altogether newe whereby it maybe termed vniuersally mixte.* Note particularly the handling of the special logical phrase *veluti pars adiuncta*, which is rendered *as a parte adioyned.* The proper names in the text of MS often take Latin forms, as in the striking case of *Flaminia*, which is the old regional name used in the Latin version to translate Romagna. Our text uses *Flaminia* up to a certain point (indicated in the notes) and then changes to *Romagna*. A sufficient number of agreements with the Latin and not with the Italian, both in the use of proper names and in the rendition of text, are given in the notes to make us safe in saying that the maker of the English translation had the Latin text at hand, indeed that it is the basal text of the English version.

The translator cannot, however, have relied solely upon the Latin. Telius does not reproduce the epistle dedicatory to Lorenzo de' Medici, and there are a sufficient number of cases in which the English translator has reproduced matter omitted from the Latin for one to be sure that the translator had also at hand a copy of a fuller text. He would hardly have been able to restore proper names to modern forms if he had not had a modern version. A question at once arises as to whether that fuller text was the original Italian or a French version of it. This matter would be easily settled were it not for the extreme freedom of the English version and the fact that Cappel's translation (1553) and the French version of Jacques Gohorry (1571), which is a reworking of Cappel, are both very close to the original Italian. Proper names are of no great assistance, since the French tends to present them in forms quite like the Italian and the English. On the whole, however, it seems probable that the English translator had a copy of the Italian, possibly Wolfe's edition (1584), which he used to supplement the Latin and to transpose most of the Italian names, but not all, back into their Italian forms. The epistle dedicatory must have come from the Italian or the French, but we are again frustrated by the extreme freedom of the English rendering. It has nevertheless seemed desirable to cite the French version of Gohorry now and then in the notes in cases in which there seems to be the possibility of the English translator's having consulted the French. It will be remembered that Gohorry's translation and Cappel's are much alike.

Something of considerable interest may be said on the origin of the Furthman manuscript, although possibly nothing definitive. As has been noted above, the quality of the handwriting in MS is excellent and is suggestive of professional training in penmanship. It had been independently suggested that certain documents from Lansdowne MS 99, namely No. 98, published by the Malone Society (_Collections_, I, 2) were in the hand of Thomas Kyd, this on the basis of the resemblance of the handwriting to that of Kyd's Letter to Sir John Puckering, the Lord Keeper, and to the articles of accusation against Christopher Marlowe contained in British Museum, MS Harley 6848.[4] It was seen at once that

[4] See W. W. Greg, _English Literary Autographs_, No. XV; _The Works of Thomas Kyd_, edited by Frederick S. Boas. Oxford, 1901, Introduction.

the handwriting of these papers in Lansdowne MS 99 bears a strong resemblance to that of the Furthman manuscript of Machiavelli's *The Prince*, but since we do not know the occasion of the challenges to the tournament in Lansdowne MS 99, or the identity of the participants, or any connection between Kyd and that enterprise, this observed resemblance serves only to suggest that Kyd might be the copyist. Further slight confirmation comes from another source.

We do not know the provenance of the Furthman manuscript, and it does not seem possible at this time to trace it with any exactitude. This manuscript, with other books and documents, came on sale in a London auction room in or about the year 1930. The lot was purchased by a London bookseller. He is of the opinion that the books and manuscripts came originally from the Vere family. He believes this on the ground that in the collection was a manuscript of the "Commentaries" of Sir Francis Vere (1560-1609), distinguished general of English forces in the wars of the Low Countries during the reign of Queen Elizabeth. This document did not come into Mr. Furthman's possession. From another source Mr. Furthman acquired, however, a copy of Lydgate's *Fall of Princes: The Tragedies, gathered by Iohn Bochas, of all such Princes as fell from theyr estates throughe the Mutability of Fortune. . . . Translated into English by John Lidgate*, London, John Wayland, [1558]. In folio. On a blank page at the end of this book there appears a transcript of Chidiock Tichborne's *Elegy*, as follows:

> My pryme of youthe is but a froste of cares
> My feast of ioye is but a tast of payne
> My crop of corne is but a fielde of tares
> And all my good is but vaine hope of gayne
> The daye is gonne and yet I sawe noe sonne
> And nowe I lyve and nowe my lyfe is done.

The spring is past and yet it hath not spronge
The fruite is deade and yet the leaves are greene
My Youth is gone and yet I ame but younge
I sawe the worlde And yet I was not seene
My threed is cutt and yet it was not sponne
And nowe I lyve and nowe my lyfe is done.

I sought for death and founde it in the wombe
I looke for lyte and sawe it but a shade
I troode the Earth and knewe it was my tombe
And nowe I dye and nowe I was but made
My glasse is full and nowe my glasse is rune
And nowe I lyve and now my lief is done.

This poem seems first to have been printed through the circumstance that Thomas Kyd in 1586 published it with a poetical reply on the heinousness of treason in a little book called *Verses of Prayse and Ioye*, on the occasion of Her Majesty's preservation from the Babington plot.[5] Kyd's version is not identical with the one just given, but his indictment of Tichborne fits the present version quite as well as it does the one he publishes. The experts consulted agree that the manuscript verses in the copy of Lydgate, not only the Elegy, but a fair copy of two of Lydgate's stanzas on a blank space at the end of the volume, are almost certainly in the same hand as the Puckering letter. If they are in the same hand as the Puckering letter, they are in Kyd's hand; and, since the hands of the verses and of the manuscript (and of the Puckering letter too, for that matter) are alike in general style and in the detailed forms of individual letters, it seems possible, that the manuscript translation of *The Prince* here published was copied by Thomas Kyd. One would say "certain" instead of possible were it not for the fact that determination of handwriting is a matter in which even great experts

[5] See *The Works of Thomas Kyd*, pp. xxv, xxvi, 339-42.

Chidiock Tichborne's *Elegy* appearing on blank
page of Lydgate's *Fall of Princes* (1558)

are of necessity very cautious and were it not for the fact also that the particular handwriting concerned in this case is a conventional, possibly a professional, hand which lacks the strong individual peculiarities in the hands of private writers.

There is another matter which might be mentioned. Among the manuscripts acquired with the translation of *The Prince* and now in Mr. Furthman's possession is an incomplete translation into English of *Aesop's Fables*. It seems to be written in the hand of Arthur Golding, who it will be remembered was uncle to the seventeenth Earl of Oxford. In this collection is a fable "Of a ffoxe & a Gote" which may supply the original for Nashe's taunt in the prefatory epistle to Greene's *Menaphon*—his mention of "the Kidde in Aesop." This allusion has been thought to be, not to *Aesop's Fables*, but to Spenser's *Shepheardes Calender*. But the fable in this copy of Aesop, although not perfectly applicable, is perhaps the best that has been found. Nashe says in the familiar passage: "The sea exhaled by droppes will in continuance be drie, and Seneca let bloud line by line, and page by page, at length must needes die to our stage: which makes his famisht followers to imitate the Kidde in *Aesop*, who enamored with the Foxes newfangles, forsooke all hopes of life to leape into a new occupation; and these men renowncing all possibilities of credit or estimation, to intermedle with Italian translations, etc." The fable follows:

Of a ffoxe & a Gote.

A Gote & a ffoxe beeing pressed with drythe of thirst, leaped downe toogether intoo a Well. The Gote considering the steepnesse of the descent, & the hard getting up ageyne, sayd he feared least he should bee taken there, & therefore did cast all the wayes he could devyse too get owt. The foxe bade him bee of good cheere; for he had already devysed a way too scape thence. Whervppon he counseled the Gote too set vp his forefeete as

hygh as he could ageynst the wall, and stowping somewhat fore-
ward with his head, too make himself as a ladder for him too get
vp. When the Gote had so doone, and the ffoxe was gotten vp
vppon the brim of the well owt of all daunger: he taunted the
vnadvysednesse of the Gote with these wurdes. Had there bin
as good store of wit in thy head, as there is of heare vppon thy
chinne, thow wouldest not have adventured so rashly intoo the
pitte, withowt considering how thow myghtest have gotten out
ageyne. *The Moralle.* It is the propertie of a wyse man, so too
wey the enteraunces consequences & issewes of thing*es* too-
gither aforehand, that he fal not intoo daunger throwgh vnad-
vysed rashnesse. Destruccion the end of deceytfull lyght
beleef. He that beleeveth hastily is lyghtmynded, & shalbee
browght lowe. Eccl: 19.4. All deceyvers are an abhominacion
too the Lord! Prou: 3. 23.

The fable is reproduced here because of its interest and its
connection with Kyd, and not because its appearance in this
lot of manuscripts is thought to have evidential value. It may
give another very slight indication that in the documents we
have been considering there are traces of the literary activi-
ties of Thomas Kyd. To prove that Kyd was the copyist of
the following translation of *The Prince* is not a matter of
great importance. It would be more important if we could
prove that he translated it or could ascertain the names of
the persons for whom he copied it. But neither of these things
is forthcoming.

THE PRINCE OF
NICHOLAS MACHIAVELL

To the righte noble Prince Lawrence sonne
of Peter de Medices Nicholas Machiavell,
Citizen & secretary of Florence,
wisheth healthe

Iᴛᴛ *hath euer ben the* Custome *emonge such as haue ben desirus to winne the favour of Princes, to presente them with thinges of great price* [1] *and rarest perfection. Ffor* [2] *asmuch doe wee studye to honour them with gyftes they loue, as to reverence them for the Magesty they beare. Hereof itt came, that to some* [3] *hath ben geuen horses, to some armours, cloth of golde to some, and to others pretious stones, to everie one such iewelles as the gevers thought meetest for theyr honours, or fittest to contente theyr humours. Searchinge therefore into the bowelles of my rychesse, beinge as ready to geeue thanckes* [4] *for benefyttes received, as to acknowledge dutye that I owe, I coulde fynde nothinge eyther for the Person your highnes beareth, more noble, or for the pollecie your Majestie oughte to vse more necessary, then the actes councells and governments* [5] *of such greate men as have susteined the offices of Kinges, and endevored to obteyne the names of* Conquerours; *they are noe ffables but truthes, seene in my tyme for the most Parte, & tryed by certeine antiquityes for the rest, which after I had collected into a small Pamphlet, I thought good to commend to your honours protection. The smallnes of the volume may perchaunce bee a hinderaunce to the greatness of the vertue. But yf it shall stande with your lykinge at idle tymes to bestowe the readinge thereof: yow shall fynde that a greater guyfte coulde not be given by soe symple a person as my self: then to lett yow vnderstande that in a shorte tyme att home in your Chamber, that I haue learned by longe experience, abroade in the worlde. And let yow gayne that with a little trowble, that I haue gotten with longe travell. I haue not labored to paynte owte these matters with Coloures, which are fitter for talles then truthes, but nakedly as truthe goeth, so to sett them owte, thynckinge the cause to commende it self, and lyke the diamonde to glyster thoughe it be not sett in golde. To excuse the presumption which happely many will accuse mee of, that beinge a private man, I shoulde intermeddle* [6] *with Princes matters, I aunsweare, that none looke higher then they that sytt lowest; for as those that iudge of the scituations of Contryes, doe place themselues on hilles, to Consider the nature of the playnes, and in valleyes to measure the heighte of mountaynes; soe that he will iudge rightlye of the peoples actions, had neede to be a prynce, and to knowe the natures of princes; it is as necessary to bee one of the People. I hope your Majestie will accept this guyfte with the lyke mynde that it is offerred, by reading whereof yow shall easilye perceave, what a fervent desire I haue to see yow reape that honour that your vertues challenge, and aspyre to that dignitie, that your fortune promisethe. And your highnes chaunce to caste your Eyes soe lowe, as to beholde my poore estate yow shall playnly perceave howe fortune withowte my deserte hath offerred me an iniury bothe infinyte and intollerable.*

ᴀ table of the Chapters conteyned in this present Booke

FINIS

THE PRINCE OF
NICHOLAS MACHIAVELL

The Prince

OF NICHOLAS MACHIAVELL

*Howe many kyndes of principalities there are, & by
what meanes they are gotten.* Cap: 1.

WHATSOEVER state of government either hath
ben, or nowe is emongst men, the same maybe called either populer where all or many beare the
swaye, or princely, where one alone hath the soveraignty. The Pryncely states doe either discende
by inheritaunce to them whose Ancestours of longe
tyme haue enioyed the diadem, or elles they are
newly gotten. These [1] laste are eyther such where-
layne was to *Frauncis Sforza*, or elles annexed as it
vnto before noe tytle coulde be pretended, as *Mil-*
were a parte of the inherited state of the Prynce that
inioyes the same; as the kyngdom of *Naples* was to
the kynge of *Spayne*. The states of government soe

3

gotten, are either accustomed to live under the obedience of a
Prynce, or free w*ith*owt controllment, and they are woonn
either by foraine force, or our owne, by fortune or vertue.

Of *principalities that discend*
by inheritaunce.   *Cap:* 2.

I WILL not discoorse of populer Estates, of these I haue
spoken more att large in an other place, I will nowe only
intreate of that state of governmente w*hi*ch Prynces haue,
and so knittinge vpp the devisions I will follow my purpose
of settinge downe howe that kynde of state may best be governed and maynteyned. Ffirst lett this[1] bee a principle, that
there is lesse difficulty for a prynce to governe Contryes dis-
cending to him by inheritance, w*hi*ch haue of long tyme ben
invred to the obedience of his progenito*ur*s, then those w*hi*ch
by any meanes he shall newly obteyne. Ffor it is sufficient
for a naturall Prince not to transgresse the lawes and orde-
nances of his Predecessors, and for the rest to vse tyme as
occasions shalbe offred. And soe may a Prynce of meane
reache in matters of state continewe alwayes in safty in his
Dominions, and if by adversaryes he be disturbed, or by
extreme force despoyled of the same, though the vsurper[2] be
never soe cumbersom, he shall notw*ith*standing recover it.
Of this in Italy the duke of *Ferrara* maybe an example,
who by noe other meanes could w*ith*stande either the assaltes
of the *Venetians* in the yeare 1484; or the invasions of Pope
Julius in the yeare 1516 [1510],[3] but only because he
had longe continewed in that kynde of govermente. Ffor
the naturall Prynce hath lesse cause to do hurte, and therefore
more reason why he shoulde be lyked, and vnlesse he incurr
the hate of his subiec*tes* by some notable & extraordinary

vice, he shalbe naturally of them beloved, & by the longe
continewance of his reygne, the memory of alteracion wilbe
cleere rased [4] & rooted owte; for alwayes the ende of a
presente chaynge leaves fit matter & good occasion for the
beginninge of an other.

Of mingled principalities.   Cap: 3.

Bᴜᴛ in a newe principality there are som combers, specially yf (as a parte adioyned it be not altogether newe
whereby it maybe termed vniuersally mixte.[1] The chaynges
& alteracions thereof seeme to springe first of that difficulty
which is commonly seene in every newe principalitye. Ffor
when men are enticed with hope of the better, they [2] gladly
wishe the innovation of that they haue: and led with
that affection, are very apte to enter into Armes against
their soueraigne, wherein [3] they are wonderfully deceaved,
for in very deede they perceave at last that they haue taken
a wronge coorse, and the cause hereof dothe happen of an
other naturall & common consequent, which causeth a
newe Prynce to offende them over whom he came lately
to raigne, aswell with charge of maintayninge his Armies,
as divers inconveniences and infinite iniuryes which followe
a newe conquest. Whereby he shall haue them his enemyes
whom he had dammaged in recovering the raigne, and yet
not certaine to keape them his ffrendes by whose meanes he
was raysed to the govermente. Ffor he can neither satisfy
their hope nor execute punishmente uppon them beinge
already beholding vnto them. Ffor let a Prynce be never soe
stronge & mighty in Armes, yet in the Conquest of a province
he shall neede the helpe and favour of the inhabitantes. These
bee the causes that *Lewes* the xii[th] kinge of *Fraunce*, lost

Millayne presently after the winninge of it, and the private force of *Lewes Sfortia,*[4] was sufficient & spare to recover it. Ffor they that were authours of his entringe of the Cyttie even they when they sawe themselues deceved of their opinion, and frustrate of the future benefitt they dreamte of, coulde not endure the trowbles and greevances of their newe [f4] Prince. And yet this is manifest that where the people haue already revolted, they are very hard to be retayned[5] when they are brought againe to subiection. Ffor vppon occasion of rebellion the Prince may more surely[6] stande vppon his garde, punishing the offendors, discovering the suspected, and fortefyinge the places[7] of lesse strength in such sorte that yf the authority of Duke *Lewes* alone blustringe in Armes aboute the ffrontyres had not then ben sufficient and more to recover the *Dukedome of Millayne* from the *french Kinge,* the wholle worlde well neere must of necessity haue conspyred against him, and his Armies must[8] haue ben overthrowne and driven owte of *Italie,* which is manifest to haue proceeded of the causes before rehersed, notwithstandinge that it was taken from him agayne the seconde tyme.

Wee haue hitherto considered the common causes of the first losse of *Millayne* by the *french kinge,* nowe it resteth that wee vnfolde the reasons why he loste it the seconde tyme, and sett downe what remmedyes he mighte haue had that tyme, and what any man might haue nowe; yf he were in the same state to defende himself in the goverment[9] better then the *French Kinge* did.

Those kyndes of states I saye which stande on these termes are either vnited to some other anciente governmente which belonges to the same Prynce that conquered them, or elles they are coupled to the same province in society, or yf they be not[10] it is a very easye matter to keepe them, specially yf the manner of theyr lyf haue not ben accustomed to libertie, and for safe possession of them, it suffisethe to extinguishe [11] the race of the prince that raigned over them before, for in other respects men live quietly together, soe their ancient lawes be not alterred and diversity of their manners reconciled; as we haue seen the *Burgundines, Brittons, Gascoynes,* and *Normans* of longe tyme consociate with *Fraunce,* for althoughe there be some difference of their languages, yet doe they all beare themselues together, very lyke in manners and forme of lyffe. But when governments are gotten in a province,[12] wherein there is difference of language, manners and lawes, there are difficulties, there are labours, there to keepe them is required greate dexteritie and singuler dilligence, and withall it is the principallest poynte of remedy for him that hath gotten them to be there both in person and abydinge, for that should make the possession more safe and permanente. As the *Turke* himself thought best to be doon in *Greece,* whoe maintayninge all their lawes to conserve that Empyre, yet had never been able to [13] keepe it excepte he had gonne and planted [14] his dwellinge there, ffor a Governour beinge presente beholdethe all tumulteous and confused Actions, & may woorke any presente redresse. In his absence he only heareth tydinges, and is advertised of the innormityes thereof. But in such tyme when all possibillity of redresse is quyte past: & further by his presence the Provynce shall never lye open to the pillage and spoyle of his Officers. Then doe the conquered people thyncke themselues satisfied, when they haue soe neere recoorse to the protection of their presente Prynce, and thereby they take the more occasion to loue him, yf they covyte to seeme loyal Subiects, otherwise they are to be dowbted yf any straynger shoulde practise to intrude [15] any such Principalitie, it shall stande him vppon to attempte it with the greater consideracion, soe yf he be residente there, he shall not lightlie be thrust from it. An other of the rediest [16] remedyes for this purpose is to send Colonies [17] as keyes into soondry partes of this iurisdiction, or ells many bandes of horsmen and footmen to be kept there. In fownd-inge Colonies the prynce is never att any greate [18] charge, either in bringinge them thither, or continewinge them there. And them [19] only doth he offende from whom he takes their landes and houses to be possest with new Inhabitantes, whoe beinge the least parte of the strength of the provynce, beinge once disperste and thrust owte in wante and poverty, can never be of power to hurte him. And then all the reste as many as are partlie free from dammage, (and therefore the easier to perswade) and partly fearinge to offende vnad-visedly, will stande in awe leste they taste the same sawce with theyr spoyled neighbours.

Wherefore I conclude that the Colonies, which bringe little charge, are more loyall & doe lesse hurte, and they that are iniured beinge nowe beggers and vacabondes, can (as I sayde before) doe noe hurte at all.[20] Besydes it is a speciall poynte of Goverment to wynne men with smooth woordes, or rowndly to cutt them of, for lighte iniuryes they revenge, but greate wronges they cannott. And therefore that abuse which is offerred a man, shoulde be such as needes not to stande in feare of revenge. But yf Garrisons of Soldiers be planted in steede of Colonies,[21] the prynce shalbe enforced to bere the greater charge because all the revenew that shoulde haue come to him of that Province must be con-sumed in maynteyninge his Garrisons, and soe that which he had gotten before, must nowe be exchaynged for losse, [f5] besydes many moe are by that meanes iniured, for the wholle province must be anoyed by dislodginge and shyftinge to and fro their Campes. With which inconvenience all the rest beinge dammaged, the Prynce purchaseth the generall hatred and mislykinge of all, whoe thoughe they be spoyled and oprest, yet remayninge in the Contry, maye haue fytt opportunity to molest and hurte him. Therefore these Garrisons of soldiers are every way vnproffitable, and Colonyes withowte dowte verie beneficiall.[22]

Furthermore it behoveth a prynce which inhabiteth any such province of contrary language, to make himself a heade & protectour of his weker [23] neighbours, and withall to devise meanes that the greater sorte maybe weakened, then let him beware that noe straynger of as greate power as himself, sett foote in the same Province,[24] for it is commonly seen that the straynger [25] is brought in by those which vpon extreme ambition, repyne att the prosperitie of the Prynce. As it is [26] manifest that in tymes past the *Romanes* were brought into *Greece* by the *Ætolians*, & what Province soever they entered they were brought thither by the inhabitantes.

Ffor it is thus provided of nature, that as soone as any strainger invades a Province, all the weker & baser sorte ioyne themselues to his syde vppon a certeyne hatred they beare those, whom they haue fownde more mighty then themselues; soe that respecting the meaner multitude, he shall neede noe great labour to drawe them to his faction, for all sortes of men are willinge to followe the conqueste. This onlye standes him vpon to looke vnto, that their strengthe and authortie doe not increase, for he beinge mighty of himself shalbe hable of his owne force, and their favours to yoke the better sorte with ease, and quickly to make himself cheef of the wholle Provynce. But this parte beinge not artificiallie handled all goes to wracke which he had gotten before, and howe longe soever he keepe it he shalbe trowbled with infinite difficultyes & trowbles.

The *Romaines* in the provinces they subdued did carefully observe these Rulles to plant Colonies,[27] defende the weake,

brydle the stronge, & to permitt noe dignitye nor prerogative, to the mightie foreiners, one only example of Greece
shall suffyce.

The *Achaians* & *Ætolians* were spared [28] by the *Romanes*
when the Realme of *Macedone* was conquered and *Antiochus* overcome. And yet neither the *Achaians* nor
Ætolians deserts coulde never obtiegne that they should
carry any stroke in the Empyre. Neither coulde they be induced by *Phillips* perswasions to embrace his amitie althoughe he weare not yet in subiection to the *Romanes*,
neither coulde they be perswaded by the power of *Antiochus*
to graunte him any authoritie in that Provynce.

In these causes of deliberacions the *Romans* did as wyse
Prynces shoulde doe, which doe not only see the occasions
of presente Ruynes, but alsoe foresee them that may ensue,
and with all care endeavour to withstande them, for beinge
longe before considered, they maye easilye be prevented
with soome remedye, but yf a man linger tell they touche
him att hande, they are paste all tymely healpe the disease
beinge nowe growen incureable.

And herein it happened as Phisitions saye in the feaver
Hectica, which when it panges any man att first, is easye to
cure, but hard to know, but not taken nor healed in tyme is
easye to know, but passinge hard to cure.[29] Soe in matters of
govermente, yf future actions bee longe before considered,
which thing indeede none but wyse men can doe, there
maybe fownde presente redresse for any incoveniences that
may aryse, but tyme beinge delayed, and they sufferred to
take roote that all men may perceaue them, there remaynes
then no possible hope of redresse. And therefore the *Romans*
foreseeinge longe before, what mischeefs might happen, did
alwayes applye present remedyes delayinge noe occasion of
warr for to withstande them; for they knewe very well that

the warres were not hereby removed from them, but rather more and more drawen vppon them; and therefore they warred in *Greece* with *Phillip* & *Antiochus*, least the other shoulde bee doinge with them in *Italie*, and yet they might haue avoyded both att that tyme, which notwithstandinge they woulde not.

Neither did they ever alowe that opinion which is common in the mouthes of all wise men of our age, that wee oughte to vse the libertie of tyme, but they always regarded what was meete for theyr peculier vertue, and wysdome, for tyme beares before it all thinges aswell good as evill, & may bringe with it as well evill as good.[30]

But to returne to *Fraunce* from whence wee degressed,[31] lett vs examyne whether *Fraunce* hath perfoormed any of these poyntes wee haue spoken, neither will I saie ought what *Charles* himself Kinge of *Fraunce* hath doon, but I will speake only of *Lewes*, the coorses of whose councells maybe better sene into, in respect of the longer possession he healde[32] in Italie, and then shall anie man playnly [f6] perceaue that whatsoeuer was to be doone for continuance of his segniorie, differinge in language, was all quyte neglected, and that he followed a clene contrarie coorse. *Lewes* throughe the ambition of the *Venetians* was brought into Italie, whoe vppon his cominge woulde haue wrested into their owne possession, the half of *Lumberdie* on this syde[33] the *Alpes*. This cominge hither of *Lewes* and the dryfte of his enterprise, I cannot discommende, for when hee beganne to putt[34] foote in *Italie*, and had no frendes in that Provynce, and perceavinge by occasion of *Charles* his affayres, that alwayes were barde him, he was driven[35] in the ende to gette such frendes as hee mighte. And trulye the successe of his devise had fallen owte to his mynde yf hee had not overshott himself in administration of the rest. Ffor the kinge himself havinge gotten

Lumberdie, he presentlie recovered that estimation and honour which *Charles* had pulled from him before. *Genua*
yelded, the *Florentines* became his frendes, the States of *Mantua* and *Ferrara*, *Bentiuoly*, maddam of *Furly*, the Lorde of
Faenza, of *Pezaro*, of *Rimino*, of *Camerino*, of *Piombino*, the
Lucænes, the *Pisanes*, the *Senesians*, all these enterteigned him
and desyred his amitye.[36] Then might the *Venesians* easily
perceave the rashnes of their owne devises: when to gayne
2 Cittyes [37] of *Lumbardy*, they made the Frenche Kynge
Lorde of the greater parte of all *Italye*.

Nowe maye any man imagine, with what small difficultie
the kinge might haue kepte his segniorye in *Italie*, yf he had
observed those rules of governmente wee haue recyted,
makinge secure and defendinge those ffrendes he had gotten,
whoe beinge somewhat manye, yet weake withall and fearinge some the Churche, some the *Venetians*, were glad to
cleaue still to his syde, and by their helpe he might soone haue
purchased himself security from the handes of them whose
power he dreaded.[38]

But he as soone as he came to *Millayne* wente cleene from
these [39] directions, assistinge Pope *Alexander* to invade *Flaminia*,[40] neither did he forsee by this coorse he shoulde
weaken himself through the losse of his ffrendes, and wante
of them which (earst for refuge) had taken sanctuary in his
bosome. Neither did he forecaste,[41] that the clergye by such
accesse of temporall Empire [42] to the spirituall iurisdiction,
woulde growe of greate power and authoritie, and havinge
committed this errour he was forced to proceede soe fare
foorthe, that to curbe the insolence of *Alexander* lest he
shoulde haue made himself Lorde over all *Tuscane*, he was
fayne himself to make a Roade into *Italie*, neither did it suffise him to haue advaunced the Clergie to that greatnes and
alienate his ffrendes from him, but on [43] Godes name he must

devyde the kingdome of *Naples* (which soe longe they thirsted [44] after) with the kinge of *Spayne*, and where he mighte haue made himself Lorde of all *Italie*, he enterteyned a *Compere* that the ambitious sorte of that Province, and such as bare him hatred mighte arme themselues with refuge vnder the wynges of his Partner. And where he mighte haue lefte some tributary kinge in the Contry, he displaced him to bringe in an other that mighte afterwardes alsoe thruste owte himself. The desyre of gettinge is a naturall and common thinge, and when men doe soe (yf they be hable [45]) it is prayse worthye, att the leaste wyse not to be blamed, but when they cannot and yet enterprise it, therein they committ greate faulte and oversyghte. Yf the *French* by their owne force had ben able to invade *Naples*, they shoulde haue doon it, yf not there was noe reason they shoulde devyde the kingdom, and if the devision of *Lumbardy* with the *Venetians* may merrite excuse because the *French* came that waye into *Italye*, yet this distribution of *Naples* deserves not to passe withowte blame by the other excuse of *Lumbardie*.

And thus did *Lewes* fall into five errours; [46] the weaker sorte he cutt of, the power of the mightie [47] he enlarged in *Italie*, hee brought in thither a most puissante mightie Prynce, he planted noe Colonies there neither wente he thither to inhabite, which errors, nothwithstandinge coulde never haue hurte him while he lived, excepte he had alsoe made the sixte faulte in cuttinge of the Venetians rule. Ffor yf he had not enlarged the power of the churche, nor brought the *Spaniardes* into Italie, then of necessity it had behoved him to haue taken them lower: but followinge these determinations he first resolued vppon, there was noe reson for him to consente to their suppression. Ffor the *Frenche* beinge mighty of themselues might easily haue repulste all others from the invasion of *Lumbardye*, and the rather because the *Venetians* woulde haue wynckte att the matter, covetinge to themselues [f7] noe iurisdiction in that dominion, and soe [48] because none elles woulde goe abowte to take itt from the *Frenche* to geeue it them. And to attempte the recouery thereof from them bothe, none woulde haue ben soe hardy: and to the former reasons I woulde aunsweare, yf any man shoulde saie that the kinge gaue vp *Flaminia* to *Alexander*, and *Naples* to the *Spaniards* to avoyde the occasion of warr: It is marvell that any man will suffer any inconvenience to avoyde warr, [49] for it is not avoyded therebye [50] but deferred to a greater disadvantage. Yf there bee any elles will alleage that the kinge gaue his faythe to the Pope to attempte that expedition att his instance, for confirmation of his owne mariage, and graunte of the redd hatt to the Legate of *Amboys*. I aunswere that obiection hereafter, where I treate of the ffaythe of Prynces, & performance thereof.

And thus did *Lewes* the *French* kinge loose *Lumbardy* when he followed not the derections which other in conqueringe and keaping provinces haue doon, neither is this straynge, but a thinge consonante to reason and very common; and of the same matter; I had conference att *Nantes* [51] with the Cardinall of *Amboys* att what tyme *Valentyne*, (for soe was *Cæsar Borgia* sonne to Pope *Alexander* called) was Lorde of *Flaminia*. And when one obiected to me that the *Italians* were rude in matters of armes, I aunswered him that the *French* were rawe in causes of Governmente, for yf they had ben experte therein, they woulde never haue lett the power of the Clergye ryse to suche greatnes, and in truthe it was manifest that the greatnes of the clergye and *Spaniards* in *Italie* grewe first from the *Frenche*, and their fall did take [52] beginninge att their advancemente. [53]

And therefore wee may gather hereof a generall & infallible position, that *The Author of an others greatnes is his owne decaye.* Ffor the author himself procurethe the power by industry or force, both which he alwayes hath in suspition that is newely aspyred to suche greatenes.

Why the Kingdom of Darius occupied by Alexander rebelled not against his successors after his death.   Cap: 4.

CONSIDERINGE the difficulties in keepinge a kingdom newly gotten, it is to be marvelled that *Alexander* conquered *Asia* in fewe yeares, and imediatelye vppon the Conquest deceassed, whereby any man might iustly imagine that all the same Empyre woulde presently enclyne to rebellion, which [1] not withstandinge, his Successers kepte wholle and fyrme to themselues, neither did they fynde any greater difficulty to preserve it but [2] what sprange emonge themselves throughe theyr vnbrydled ambition. I aunsweare that Principalities (whose conquestes are yet freshe in memory) are governed by twoe soondry wayes, eyther by a Prynce, and such as by his speciall favour (thoughe by byrthe they be inferiour persons and men of noe reputacion) are chosen to assiste him in the Goverment of the Comon wealthe, or by a prynce and certeine Peeres whoe haue ben raysed to that honour not by the favour or permission of their prynce, but by the discente and antiquitie of their owne blud. Such Peeres enioye certeine Iurisdictions, and haue people at Comandement whoe acknowledge them for their good Lordes and reverence them with a naturall kynde of allegeance. But the *prince* doth raigne with a farr greter preheminence over those principalities that are governed by the direction of one only prynce, and assistaunce of such inferiour Persons as he hath made choyse of. Ffor there is noe man in the wholle Province that will acknowledge any other superio*ur* but only the Prynce and yf he yelde allegeance to any other it is as to a deputy or Leeftenante, w*i*thout any peculier affection to the p*er*son: of these two sundry kind*es* of gov*ern*me*nt* in our age, the turke & french kinge ar most [3] lively examples. The administrac*i*on of the Turkishe Empyre standes vppon the wholle swaye and disposition of one only soveraigne, the reste are att his co*m*maunde. And his Empire beinge devided into many [4] Leeftenantshipp*es*, he appoynt*es* divers Governo*ur*s and [5] doth depose and establishe them at his pleasure.[6] But the French kynge standes in the myddes [7] of the anciente multitude of his peeres whom the people knowe and reverence. They holde their prerogative w*h*ich the kinge himself cannott take from them w*i*thout daynger, and therefore he that considers the ma*n*ner of bothe these Governmen*tes*, shall fynde greate difficulty in attemptinge the conquest of the Turkes Empyre; but once overcominge the Turke himself it is the least matter of twenty to keepe it.

The reasons [8] why the Turkes Empyre is harde to be woon are, [f8] because he that shall enterpryse it, shall neither bee called in by the Peeres nor can conceave any hope that they whoe are nere the Prynce will revolte from their alegeance, w*h*ich seeme [9] to proceede of the causes before rehersed. But [10] in as much as they are all his Vassell*es*, and beinge bownde to him in allegeance, they are the harder to be corrupted, there were small hope notw*i*thstandinge to doe any good because they cann never leade the people w*i*th them, for the causes before alleaged. And therefore he that will haue a sayinge to the Turke must imagine to fynde him resollute and to be conquered rather w*i*th his owne puissance, then by seditions and discord*es* of others, but he him self beinge once overthrowne and foyled in the fylde, that he cannot recover his Armye, there is nothinge to be feared afterwarde, but the bloud and ofspringe of the Prynce, which beinge once extinguished, there is noe man then to bee dowbted, all the Turkishe Captaines beinge voyde of Countenaunce and authoritye. And as before the conquest there was noe hope for the victor to drawe them to his syde, soe after the conqueste there is as little reason wherefore he shoulde feare them. But is is farr otherwise in kyngdomes governed lyke *Fraunce*, for into those it is easy for any man to enter, that is assisted with any of the Cheefe Peeres, for alwayes there are some emongst them, whoe livinge malcontent*es* [11] in mynde, doe therefore labo*ur* after innovation. And by the former reasons are able to open the passage [12] to that kyngdom and make farr more speede in the conquest, in keepinge whereof afterward*es*, there are notwithstandinge a nombre of difficulties not only with thy assistant*es* but alsoe with them whom thowe hast Conquered. Itt sufficethe not to haue destroyed the Princes race only whereas the principall peeres are yet remayninge which will make themselues authors of newe alteracions, whom when thow canst neither satisfye nor cutt of, thow shalbe forste to forgoe the principalitie as soone as euer tyme present*es* oportunitie. Nowe yf thow consider the manner howe *Darius* his kingdome was governed att that tyme, thow shallt fynde it very like vnto the Turkes; and therefore it stoode *Alexander* vppon to attempt it with might and mayne,[13] and to hoyse Darius owte of his tentes, after which conquest *Darius* disceasing the Empyre came entirely and peaceably vnto him by the reasons before alleaged.[14] And his successors, yf they had continewed in concorde, might att pleasure haue enioyed it, for never any tumulte happened in it but what they raysed themselues; But those Principalityes that followe the *French* government are impossible to be possest with lyke quietnes, for hence grewe the often rebellions of *Spayne*, *Fraunce*, & *Greece*, from the *Romanes* because the power of the *potentates* was passinge greate in those provinces, of whose ancient lyues [15] as long as memorie lasted the *Romans* were alwayes vncertaine of the possession of their Provinces.

But the remembraunce of them beinge worne owte by the reputacion and continewaunce of the Empyre, lyke secure persons they enioyed secure possession. And afterwarde accordinge to every mans estimation, by the Provinces he conquered (yea though they fell to civill iarre) was he hable to bringe assistaunce in defence of his parte. And the rather because the race of their former prince beinge extinguished thencefoorth they acknowledge noe Soveraigne but the *Romans*.

These thinges considered lett noe man marvell that *Alexander* did soe easily preserue the principallitie in *Asia*, neither lett him woonder att the difficulties which manie Princes haue fownde (as Pirhus and divers other [16]) in keapinge and defendeing what before they had conquered, for that falles owte not by the greate or small vertue of the Conquerour but by occasion of vnlyke qualletyes and diversity of the matter.

Howe cittyes and Segniories ought to be gouerned which were accustomed to liue after theyr owne Lawes and Libertye.   *Cap: 5.*

IN A DOMINION woon by conquest where the people haue lived after the aunciente custome att liberty and theyr owne appoyntment, in them there are three meanes to continewe the righte of a mans possession, first vtterly to subvert and destroye the cheeffe cittye, secondly to goe and inhabitt there, lastly to lett them live after their owne lawes and liberties in respecte thereof exactinge only some annuall tribute, and withall thow must substitute some fewe Governours vnder thee to keepe it in allegeaunce, whoe beinge once placed there, (and knowinge that they cannot continewe withowte the good grace and countenaunce of the Prynce) will doe their vttermost indevour to preserve his superoritie. Ffor example, wee haue the *Spartanes* and *Romanes*, the *Spartanes* conquered *Athens*, and *Thebes*, and havinge sett a fewe governours there, loste bothe the Citties notwithstandinge. The *Romans* sackte *Capua, Carthage* & *Numantia*, and by [f9] that meanes loste them not, *Grece* they attempted to keepe as the *Spartans* did, but permittinge them the libertye of their owne lawes, the matter fell not owte aunswerable to their driffte, soe that for quiet possession thereof, they were fayne to destroye many Citties in the Province. And therefore there canbe noe better devise for secure possession of them then to destroye the Cittye. Ffor hee that becomes Lorde of a Cittye, which hath ben accustomed to live after their owne lawes, must either ditermine to overthrowe the citty, or to make reconinge that the Cittie shall overthrowe him: for in tyme of rebellion, they haue always scope of refuge, and that is to their owne anciente orders, which neither by continewaunce of tyme, nor deserte of good tourns canbee forgotten: for the inhabitaunce [1] beinge not yet disvnited nor dispersed, the sweete name of liberty and their former lyffe can never fall owte of their remembraunce, but in all States and coorses of tyme, they flie thither as to the fynall and laste refuge, as wee haue seene the *Pysanes* doe after soe many yeares to avoyde that servitude wherein the *Florentines* had yoked them. But these Cittyes or provinces, that haue ben accustomed to the obedience of a Prince whose race is vtterly extincte, cannot conceive what it is to live att libertie,

whereby they are nothing soe forwarde to enter into armes.
And them, maye the newe Prynce drawe the more easilye
to his allegeaunce, and live secure of any sinister attemptes,
for partely they haue ben accustomed to obey, and partlie
(their owne Prynce beinge loste) they will agree emonge
themselues to choose some other in his place, where contrarywise the free Citties, that haue lived att liberty, will
keepe in their myndes a perpetuall hatred against such as
haue brought them into ² subiection with a continewall desire
of revenge. For ³ the anciente memory of their libertie will
never suffer them to live in subiection quietlie, wherefore the
surest waye is to sacke their cittie and vtterly destroy them,
or ells for the Prynce to goe and inhabite emongste them.

Of newe principalities which are gotten by proper strength and Vertue.   Cap: 6.

L ETT it not seeme strainge yf in discoorsinge of principalities newly gotten, I bringe in the examples of Princes
and greate Estates, for men commonly in theyr proceedinges
followe the beaten pathes and imitate the verteous actions
of such as haue gon before. And ¹ thoughe they cannot exactly treade theyr steppes or fully reache to their vertues,
yet is it the parte of a wise man to haue an eye to the best and
imitate him nighest that did exell moste, soe yf he cannot at-
teigne to the perfection ² of his vertues yet shall hee haue att
leaste some taste of his glorye, followinge the example of
cunninge Archers, whoe intendinge to shoette att a marke
that is beyonde their reache knowinge the strength of their
bowe, & howe farr it will carrye, doe take a higher compasse
then otherwise woulde serve, not that they meane by that
proportion to overshoote the marke, but knowinge the

weakenes of their bowe make shewe to shoote over, that att
the least they maye shoote home. And touchinge the kepinge
and continewance of principalities newly gotten, I am of
opinion that the difficulties therof are either more or lesse,
accordinge as the vertues of the geetter [3] or Conqueror, be
either greate or small. This strainge evente when a meane and
private man is raysed to the dignity of a Prynce, doth pre-
suppose either some excellent vertue, or woonderfull fortune
in the Winner, both which doe mittigate the difficulties that
are incident to the keepinge of suche estates, howe be it he that
leaneth least vppon the favour of fortune standeth surest, and
is lyke to continewe longeste. The necessitie that such a
prince hathe to dwell in his newe gotten territory, havinge
noe other dominion to call him away dothe make the difficulties lesse, his presence takinge awaye the occasions of
manye inconveniences.

But to come to those which by their owne vertue, and
not by fortunes healpe haue ben advanced to the state of
princes, I thincke Moyses, *Cyrus, Romulus,* and such lyke
were the cheeffeste, and although we are not [4] to speake here
of *Moyses,* (whoe onlye executed those thinges precisely
which were prescribed him by the devine power of Godd,)
yet maye wee [f10] greatlie [5] wonder att the favour he receaved in that he was thoughte woorthy to talke with godd,
but yf wee consider the lyffe of *Cyrus* and others that were
fownders of their owne Empires, wee shall fynde them
woorthy of greate admiration, and comparinge their Actions
and perticuler ordinances with those of *Moyses,* who had
for his directour soe greate and soveraigne a Guyde, yow
shall perceve but little difference; for examininge their noble
actes [6] with the wholle course of their lives, it will appere
that they had nothing given them by the favour of fortune,
but only occasion which yelded them fitt matter whereby

they might bringe in what manner of government they thought conveniente. Withowte such occasion their vertue had ben smoothered, and never sett a woorke. And [7] had they wanted vertue to haue taken the oportunity, the occasion had ben offerred in vayne. Itt was therefore necessary for *Moyses* that the Children of *Israell* shoulde be captive in Egipte, and that they shoulde be oprest by the *Egiptians*, that yf they woulde seeke to drawe their neckes owte of that servile yoake of bondage, they shoulde haue a desyre to followe him as their Captaine. It was convenient for *Romulus* that he was not receved into *Alba*, but euen from his birthe to be throwen owte as a praye vnto wylde beastes that afterwarde he might enioye the Empire of Rome [8] and be the fownder of soe greate a Cittye. Itt was agreable to the fortune of *Cyrus* that he shoulde fynde the *Pertians* displeased with the Governmente of the Medes,[9] and the *Medes* softe and effeminate throughe their longe Peace and quietnes. *Theseus* had noe meanes to exercise the vertues of his noble mynde, yf he had not fownde the *Athenians* wanderinge and dispersed. These occasions made these men happy and the vertues of theyre myndes tooke the benefytt of the tyme, and made the occasions knowen and perceaved, whereby their Contrie became famous, and themselues fortunate. Those which by such verteous wayes as these, becom Prynces, clymbe hardly to their estates, but keape it with greate quyetnes. The difficulties which are incidente to the keapinge and continewance of a newe gotten principalitie doe rise partlie from the Lawes Statutes and ordinances which the Prince shalbe forced to make for the saftie of his owne estate. Ffor this is to be noted that there is nothinge soe harde to enterprise nor soe dowbtefull to ende, nor soe dayngerous to proscecute as to make a mans self Author of newe lawes or customes. For [10] he that is the first bringer in of them shalbe

sure to haue all those his Enemyes that reaped any com-
moditye by the olde and those but his colde frendes that hope
for any proffitte by the newe which coldnes dothe springe
partlie for feare of their adversaries to whom the olde lawes
were beneficiall, and partlie throughe mens incredulitie,
which will never certeinly beleue any thinge to come vnlesse
they see it confirmed by manifest experience. Hereof it
comes that when the mislikers haue any occasion of resistaunce offered, they doe it violently, and the favorers
defende it coldlye, soe that they all runn into dainger together. To make this playne wee must first consider whether
these newe lawe makers doe relye only vppon them selues,
or depende vppon the healpe of others; that is to saye in
bringinge their purpose to effecte,[11] whither they shalbe
driven to request the conscente of others, or be [12] hable to
enforce them to agree. Yf [13] the first, it never falles owte well,
neither doe they bringe any thinge to effect, but where they
relie on themselues, and maye constrayne those that mislyke,
there is seldom or never daynger of good successe. Hereof it
came that the proffettes that wee spake of, that were hable
to enforce were alwayes Conquerours, and the other which
had noe power were continewally martered. Ffor better
proffe hereof wee must note, that the myndes and opinions
of men, are naturaly variable [14] & vnconstante, easilye perswaded to beleeue any newe doctrine: but hardly keapt to
continewe in that beleef; therefore the matter must be soe
handled, that when theyr fayth [15] fayles, force maye take
place and force them to perfoorme that by violence, that
they vndertooke with their conscentes. *Moyses, Cyrus,*
Theseus, Romulus, yf they had wanted force to confirme
their decrees, coulde never haue made their constitutions to
haue continewed of any force amonge their [f11] People as
it fell owte of late with ffryer *Hierominus Sauonarolonus,*

whoe fell to vtter ruyne with all his newe Ceremonyes, soe soone as he wanted power to confirme such as had once received his opinions, & to cause such as were incredulus to beleue perforce. Wherefore such men as attempte such [16] kynde of invasion, fynde greate difficulty in their enterance, and some in proceedinge, but all the daynger (which by their vertue they must overcome) consistes [17] in the right administringe of such newe decrees, but havinge once past that, & beinge crepte into creaditt emonge the multitude, they shall alwayes remayne mightie, (withowt perrill) in greate honour and safetie. To those highe & famous examples, I will adde one of meaner recominge, and yet shall haue some liklihood & proportion with these that wente before, & that shalbe of *Hieron* [18] *Seracusanus*, he of a private man became prince of the *Seracusans,* havinge nothinge to thancke fortune for, but onlye occasion; for the *Seracusanes* beinge oppressed chose him for the Captaine, which proved that he deserved to be their prynce, he was of soe rare vertue in his private fortune, that they which did wryte [19] of him doe affirme that he wanted nothinge to be a kinge, but a kingdom. He [20] chaynged the olde disciplyne of warres, & framed newe, he brake of olde leagues, and confirmed newe with others, and soe havinge ffrendes, and Soldiers of his owne choyce, and in his owne power, he was hable to buylde vppon this fowndacion what he thoughte good. Soe that he endured great Labour in gettinge, and small payne in keepinge of his Principalitie.

Of those which haue gotten newe principalities either by the ayde of other men or their owne fortune.   *Cap:* 7.

Svche as of private men becom princes only by the benefitt of fortune, come easilie by their soveraigntie, but hardlie continewe their safetie,[1] in atteininge the one they fynde smale difficultie, because they come by it on the sodaine, but in meynteininge the other greate daynger, because tymes[2] breedes trowbles, and such are they as haue been raysed to the highe typ of honour either by their owne wealthe, as it hath happened to divers private men amonge the *Romans,* whoe by corruptinge the soldiers became Emperours, or other mens liberalitie as wee finde it hathe chaunced to divers in the Cytties of *Greece, Ionia* & *Hellesponte,* where *Darius* made many Princes, and indued them with greate Segniories[3] aswell for his safetie as glorye.

The state and welfare of both these sortes of Princes depende vppon the favour and fortune of those that did advaunce them. Things[4] withowt dowbte both vnstable and vnconstante and vnfitt proppes to support soe greate a weighte, and therefore vnlesse such a prince be indued with singuler wytte, and great vertue, (havinge benn all days of his lyffe a private man) it is impossible that he should knowe howe to governe, neither indeede can he, for he shall wante those thinges whereof he standes in most neede, force & frendship. Moreover these states as are soe quicklie gotten, can noe more then other naturall thinges that springe on the sodaine, take soe deepe Rootes or florishe in such sort,[5] but that they wilbe overthrowne with the verie first blaste of adversse fortune, vnles as it is already sayde, the princes that are raysed to such highe estate, excell soe in vertue, that they knowe presentlie howe to mannage their affayres in such manner that they cann defende and maintaine that by their wisdome, which is throwen into their bosome by fortune; and indevour carefullye to observe those rulles which others before they were kinges sett downe for Principles.

Touchinge those twoe wayes (ffortune and vertue) whereby a private man maybe raysed to the state of a prince,[6] I will heere bringe twoe examples chauncinge within the compasse of our memories, the one of *Frauncis Sfortia*, the other of *Cæsar Borgia*, *Sforzia* vsinge meanes requisite for soe greate an enterprise, by singular vertue advanced him self to be duke of *Millaine*, and was hable to defende that with smalle coste, which he had gotten with greate care. Contrariwise *Cæsar Borgia* (who was commonly called *Valentinus*) althoughe he vsed all the dilligence that possiblie he coulde, and perfoormed all those partes that a wise and a valiante man shoulde, to establish his estate in the dominions, which by armes and his father Pope *Alexanders* fortune he had atchived; yet [7] notwithstandinge he fell from all to his greate greeffe, together with his ffathers fortune that raised him to that glorie. He whoe hath not layed for his state a good fowndacion att the firste, maye (as it is sayde) by singuler vertue (thoughe not without greate difficultie) provide [8] for the same afterwarde; yf therefore wee call to mynde the proceedinges of Prince *Valentinus*, it will playnlie appeare what sufficiente grownde he layed for the continewaunce of his Estate, which are well [f12] woorthe the notinge; for I knowe not what better preceptes maybe geven a newe Prynce then to sett before his Eyes the examples of his Actions, and yf the order that he tooke for his affayres wroughte not the effect which he looked for, itt is not to be imputed to the insufficiencye of the man, but to the extreame malice of fortune. Pope *Alexander* the vj[t] endevoringe to make his soonne greate hadd his mynde perplexed with a worlde of trowbles, aswell iminente as lykly to ensue. Ffirste he sawe noe meanes to advaunce him to any principalitie, that was not appropriated by the *Sea* of *Rome*,[9] and if he wente about to pull any thinge from the churche, he knewe neither the Duke of *Millaine* nor the *Venetians* woulde suffer him, and then were *Fauentia* and *Ariminum*[10] vnder the protection of the *Venetians*; besydes that he perceaved the strengthes and Armes of *Italie*, and those which might closely[11] serue his owne turne, to be in their handes which had cause to feare the Popes greatnes, and therefore durst not trust them all be-inge vnder the commaunde of the ffamilies of the *Vrsines* & *Columnians*, and their followers, which inforced him to de-vise howe to sowe discorde[12] emonge theis confederates, and raise trowbles throughoute all *Italie*, thereby to make himself Lorde over soome parte thereof, which was easily brought to passe, for he fownde the *Venetians* moved vppon some other occasions already, but to bringe the frenchmen into *Italie*, which he hyndered not, but rather ffurthered by a constitution which[13] he made touchinge kinge *Lewes* his mariage. The *French* kinge by the help of the *Venetians* and Pope *Alexander*, came into *Italie*, and *Valentinus* came noe sooner to *Millayne* but that he obteigned a power of the kinge with full authoritie to subdue the countree of *Ro-magnia*,[14] which beinge once gotten, and the *Calumnians* vanquished: *Valentinus* havinge a desire not only to keape that, but alsoe to aspire yf he coulde possiblie to greater mat-ters, fownde twoe thinges which seemed to crosse him, his owne armie which he thought vnfaithfull, and the French kinge his favour which he knewe inconstante. He feared leste the power of *Vrsines* (which all this whyle stood him in good[15] steede) woulde nowe flynch from him, and not only hynder him in his further Conquest*es*, but be a meane to hurte him in that w*h*ich he had alreadie gotten, and he dowbted leaste the kinge woulde serue him w*i*th the same sawce. The *Vrsines* confirmed his suspytion by the colde service they shewed att the assaulte [16] of *Bononia;* after the subduinge of *Fauentia*, and what favo*u*r the kinge did beare him, did then appeere, when he havinge gotten the dukedome of *Vrbane* and ready to invade *Tuscan* was called from that enterprise by the king*es* co*m*maundemente.

Herevppon *Valentinus* [17] determined with him self to depende noe longer either vppon the inconstancie [18] of fortune, or the vncerteintie of other mens forces,[19] wherefore he begann to weaken the faction of the *Vrsines* & *Calumnians* att *Rome:* alluringe all such Gentlemen of *Rome* as tooke their partes w*i*th great stipendes and offices accordinge to eache mans deserte to revolt and followe him. In soe much that w*i*thin a smalle tyme, the affection that they had to their leaders was converted whollye to *Valentine*, w*h*ich beinge doon, he soughte occasion howe he mighte overthrowe the *Vrsines*, (havinge alreadie dispersed the power of *Columnians*) w*h*ich being happely offered, was more luckely putt in execution. The *Vrsines* perceavinge nowe thoughe to late that the risinge of *Valentinus* and the Pope, would bee their vtter ruyne: helde a Councell att *Magio del Paragino* [20] whereof did springe the rebellion of *Vrbine*, the tumullt*es* in *Romania*, and a thousande perrill*es* to Duke *Valentine*, all the w*h*ich he overcame by *th*e helpe of the frenchmen, and havinge recovered his former reputation,[21] mistrustinge the frenchmen and other foreine forces, (to keepe himself the better owte of their dainger) he bente his mynde altogether to frawde and dissimulation, and coulde soe well Cloke his crafte; that the *Vrsines* by the meanes of *S: Paulus*, reconsiled themselves vnto him, towardes which *Paulus* he omitted noe

courtesie of a frende nor dutye of a kinseman, whereby he
might wyn his hearte geving him apparrell, horses, & mony.[22]
Soe their symplicity that feared noe slyghte brought them
within his dainger att *Senogallia* to be slayne.

Thus havinge gotten the lives of those that were principall
and gayned the loues of them that tooke their partes, havinge
conquered the province of *Romania*, and subdued the duk-
dome of *Vrbine*, and woonn the heart*es* of the people, whoe
had never tasted as they thought a more happie kinde of
governmente: he layed a sufficient fowndac*i*on, for the continewance of his estate; here I will not skipp over a matter
well worthy to be observed and imitated. After that *Valentinus* had gotten the province of *Romagnia* and fownde that
it had before ben governed by certeine poore Lord*es*, w*h*ich
did rather spoyle their wealth then correct their vice, and
sowed discorde when they shoulde haue planted vnity, by
that meanes fillinge the wholle province w*i*th theftes,
brawles, and insolencyes,[23] he determined to establish and
sett downe emongst them a civill kynde of government,
whereby he mighte make the contrie more peaceable to
enioye their wealthe, and the people more tractable to obeye
their Prince: for this purpose he placed emonge them one
Remerus [f13] *Orcus*,[24] a man noe more readye to attempte
then [25] cruell to execute his purpose, to whom he gaue soveraigne authoritie. This [26] man in shorte space (to his greate
commendac*i*on) planted in that Province Peace, & Tran-
quility, but the Duke perceaved that this absolute authoritie
of his Deputy stood not well w*i*th his safetie, fearinge that it
woulde breede hatred in the heart*es* of the Co*m*monaltie,
and therefore (to prevent that mischeef) he erected in the
midst of that Province a place of Iudgment for all civill
causes, appoyntinge one of greate skill to be Presedente,
where everie Citye of the Province should [27] haue an Advo-

cate & Atturney. Yet fynding that there remayned some
sparkes of hatred in their heart*es* against him by the meanes
of the others cruelltie, that he might the better quench the
remembrance thereof,[28] cleere himself, and wynn their
heart*es*, he gave owte, that whatsoever rigo*ur* was co*m*mitted in the Province, it was not by his consente, but by the
cruell nature of his Deputie,[29] and to manifest the same, (takinge an occasion) he caused his headd to be smitten of in the
morninge in the midste of the markett Place of *Cesanea*.
This cruell sighte on the sodaine satisfied the Peoples humo*ur*[30] and amazed theire myndes. But to returne to our
purpose when the duke sawe his strength sufficientlie encreased, and himself in a ma*n*ner free from those presente
p*e*rrill*es* that might putt him in feare, havinge (as he thought)
both increased his owne strength, and weakened theirs,
w*h*ich (being his neighbo*ur*s) might offende him: it was
requisyte (yf he mente to enlarge his dominions) to haue an
eye to the french w*h*ich might hynder the coorse of his enterprise, for he knewe well enoughe that the kinge havinge to
late perceved his erro*ur* woulde hardlie yeelde to further
inconvenience. Wherevppon he beganne to seeke newe
frendes,[31] and to dallie w*i*th the Frenche in the iourney they
took to Naples, againste the *Spaniards* w*h*ich beseeged
Caietta, and to cast abowte howe he might ridd himself owte
of their dainger, w*h*ich noe dowbte hadd taken good successe[32] hadd not *Alexander* the Pope died in the meane
tyme. These were the plott*es* he layed, and practises he used
touchinge the affayres[33] he had presentlie in hande, but
concerninge afterclapp*es* he stood in dowbte, whether he
that shoulde succeed pope, would prove his frende, or cutt
him shorte of that his ffather had geeven him, but fower
wayes he practised to ridd himself of these feares,[34] first of
all by rootinge owte the wholle state of nobillitie, w*h*ich he

had any way iniured, thereby to prevente the pope of all occasion, why he shoulde revenge their wronges, secondlie by winninge the heartes of the Nobillitie of *Rome*, by their meanes to restraine and weaken the Popes power, yf att any tyme he rose against him; thirdlie by curriinge favo*ur* by all meanes he coulde devise with the college of *Cardinalls* to make them his frendes, & bynde them vnto him, lastlie by enlarginge soe farr the bowndes of his Empyre before his ffathers deathe, that thereby he might of himself be of sufficient power even att the first to resyst any forreine force or invasion. Three of these he had brought to full effect before the deathe of pope *Alexander* his father and had almost perfoormed the fowerthe,[35] for all the nobillitie that he had iniured verie fewe escaped his handes, but that they were putt to deathe, he had alsoe woon the heartes of the nobillitie of *Rome*, and gotten the goodwilles of most parte of the Cardinalls and to enlarge his Empire he purposed to make himself Lorde of *Tuscane*, having already *Perugia* and [*Piombino*] [36] vnder his subiection, and *Pisa* in his protection, and as thoughe he had noe more neede to feare the Frenchmen as is truthe he had not, the Spaniardes [37] havinge driven them owte of the kingdom of *Naples*, and bothe nations willing to purchase his frendship, he was soe bolde to take *Pisa* for his owne. After this *Luca*, & *Sienna* aswell for hatred they did beare the *Florentines*, as the feare they had of the *Duke*, yelded themselues to him, soe were the *Florentines* in a verie hard plighte, yf these thinges hadd chaunced before, as indeede they fell owte the verie yeare that pope *Alexander* died, he had made himself of that strengthe and reputacion that his owne power woulde haue ben of sufficient force to vpholde and defende himself not relyinge vppon fortune or the ayde of other men.

But Pope *Alexander* died the vth yeare after he begann his conquest, leaving him nothing certeine but the province of *Romagnia*,[38] the rest dowbtfull himself sicke of a dayngerus disease & invironed with the Armies of twoe mightie princes that were his Enemyes. The Duke was of soe noble a currage and soe full of *Valure* and knewe so well by what meanes the heart*es* of men are woon and loste, and had soe substantially in that shorte space layed his fowndac*i*ons, that had he not been opprest with those twoe Armies [39] and deprest with the extremities of his sicknes,[40] he had past the pykes & escaped [f14] all the dayngers. This [41] proves that his fowndacions were good, first the Province of *Romania* (notwithstandinge all thes broiles) helde with him more then a monethe in his sicknes he was saffe in *Rome*. And although the Baglians [42] the *Vitilians* and the *Vrsines* came thither, yet was there noe man that woulde take their partes or make head againe thoughe they sawe him in a ma*n*ner dead. And [43] although he coulde not healpe him to be Pope that [44] he lyked, yet coulde he hynder any man that he lyked not, and yf he had had his healthe when Pope *Alexander* died, he had brought his purpose to effect, and putt all owte of controversye. I remember he tolde me the same tyme that Iulius the seconde was chosen Pope that he had carefullie forecast all [45] inconvenienc*es* that might happen him by the deathe of his ffather, and had for everie mischeef provided a remedye, onlie this he dreamed not of, that when his father died he him self shoulde be in the lyke daynger.

When I therefore way and consider with my self breefly the reasons of all the Dukes proceedinges, I cannot fynde any thinge wherein I may reprehende him, but rather (as I sayde) sett him downe as a patterne to be imitated and followed of all those that either by fortune or frendship aspyre to the dignitie of a Prince; for carryinge soe highe a mynde and soe noble a coorrage, and intendinge to aspyre to soe great matters, he coulde not otherwise order his affayres then he did, onlie his fathers death and his owne sicknes hindered the perfectinge & consummation thereof. He therefore that beinge newlie advaunced to the state of a prynce, shall thincke it necessarie to fortifye himself against his Enemyes, and to purchase frendes to conquer either by frawde or force, to be beloved and feared of his subiect*es*, followed and reverenced of his soldiers, to cutt of those that maye doe hurte, and cherishe those that maye doe good; to alter olde customes by newe devises, to be severe and covetous, valiaunte and liberall, to discarde vnfaithfull soldiers and enterteine those that are trustie, soe to enter in league with king*es* and princ*es*, that they shalbe gladd to please, or att least loath to offende. In mine opinion I can fynde noe more livelye examples to expresse them in their kyndes [46] and sett them foorth in their coollo*urs*, then the Councell*es* and actions of this noble Duke *Valentinus*, in this onlie it seemes he overshott himself that he tooke not asgood coorse in sufferinge *Julius* the seconde [47] to be chosen Pope. For in that election yf [48] the lott had not lighted vppon him that he favored; he might at leaste, (as I saide before) haue fownde meanes to crosse him that he mistrusted, in anie case he shoulde not haue endured, that either of any of those Cardinall*es* should be made Pope whom he before had iniured, or any such as beinge raysed to that dignitie should haue iuste cause to feare him for men practise mischeef aswell for feare as for hatred. The Cardinall*es* whom he had offended, emonge these was he of *St. Peter ad Vincula* & *Columini*us the Cardinall of *George* & *Ascanius*,[49] all the rest that were like to be advanced to the Papall dignitie exceptinge *Rotoman*us,[50] and the *Spaniards* shoulde haue iuste cause to feare him, some because they were his kinsemen and bownde to him by many benefitt*es*, other dowbtinge his greatnes because of his alliau*n*ce with Fraunce.

Valentinus therefore should haue employed his vttermost
force to haue chosen a *Spaniarde* pope, which yf he coulde
not haue compassed he shoulde then haue bent [51] all his force
to choose *Rotomanus* by noe meanes consentinge to the ad-
vancement of Cardinall *T:D Petri ad Vincula* for he is verie
much deceaved that thinckes newe benefittes can cause
greate Lordes to forgett olde iniuryes. *Valentinus* therefore
was much overseene in that election which was the cause of
his vtter ruyne and destruction.

Of those which by wicked meanes haue gotten principalities.   Cap: 8.

NOWE for asmuch as a private man may becom a Prince
twoe wayes which cannot properlie be attributed to
fortune or vertue, I thought good not to overslipp them,
though the one maybe handled more aptlye, when wee shall
haue occasion to entreate of common welthes,[1] these twoe
wayes are ether when a man clymbes to the dignity of a
prince by some wicked or damnable practise or elles where
one Cittizen by the favour or furtheraunce of the rest becomes Prince of his Contrie. In discoursinge[2] of the first
waye I will onlie vse twoe examples, the one anciente the
other within Compasse of our owne memorie which I thincke
will yeeld sufficient instructions to such as by necessitie haue
occasion to imitate or putt them in practise. *Agathocles*[3] the
Cicilian not only beinge a private man, but alsoe of an abiect
and base Condicion became kinge of *Seracusa*, this gallaunte
beinge the sonne of a potter, throughoute all the degreesse
of his ffortune [f15] continuallie led a most wicked and vyle
lyffe. Yet he accompanied his vices with soe many good
partes of bodie and mynde, that bendinge himself towardes[4]

the warres he rose there by degresse [5] to be Pretour of *Seracusa*, in which estate he was noe sooner setled, but streight he ditermined to becom [6] their Prince, and to holde that (whether they would or noe,) which was grawnted him by all their consentes, he imparted his Councell with *Amilcar* of *Carthage*, whoe then had charge of an armie in *Sicilia*, and one morninge he caused the people and *Senate* of *Seracusa* to be called together as thoughe he mente to debate some greate matter with them touchinge the Estate,[7] & Common wealthe, where [8] (sodainlie att a watchwoord geeven his soldiers) he caused them to kill all the *Senators*, and welthiest Commoners, which beinge doon [9] accordinge to his Commaunde, he enioyed the Soveraigntie of that Cittie withowte controllment, and heald it withowte resistance, and although he was twise overthrown by the *Carthagenians*, and att lengthe beseeged within his owne walles, yet was he hable to withstande their force, and leavinge parte of his *Army* to defende the Cittie, wente with the reste and invaded *Affrica*, and soe contrived his matters, that in shorte space he both raysed the seege from *Seracusa*, and brought the *Carthagenians* into a narrowe streighte; concludinge a peace with them in the ende with these Condicions, that they shoulde contente themselues with their dominions in *Affrica*, and suffer him with quietnes to enioye the wholle Contree of *Sicillia*. Hee that will weighe the reasons and consider the coorse of this mans Actions, shall fynde therein [10] little or nothinge that maybe attributed to fortune, for asmuch as he was not raysed to this estate by the frendshipp of other men, but passinge the pykes through a thousande perrilles aspyred therevnto by degresse of millitarie discipline, refusinge afterwarde noe dainger nor omitting any dilligence for the preservation and continewaunce of his estate & [11] safetye. Neither can wee call it vertue to murther his

Cittyzens, to betraye his ffrendes, to be w*i*thout faythe, pittie and religion, by these meanes a man may obteigne a kingdome, but never attaine to glorie. Yf wee consider onlie the noble and forwarde mynde of *Agathocles*, in attempting greate matters, his value and wisdome in atchiving the same, his greate coorrage to endure hardnes, and his wonderfull fortune to escape dainger; I see noe reason why wee may not compare him w*i*th the worthiest Captaines that ever haue ben: [12] notw*i*thstandinge his brutishe ma*n*ners, and cruell nature accompanied w*i*th other infinite and most wicked vices, doe not p*er*mitt that he should be regestred emonge the Companie of verteous Princes, by this it appeares that the Principalitie w*h*ich he gott by these wicked meanes, cannot properlie bee attributed to fortune and much lesse to vertue.

The other example of later memorie chancinge in the tyme of Pope *Alexander* the vi[th] is this. [13] *Oliuer* of *Firmo* beinge lefte an Orphan, was broughte vpp from his tender yeares by *John Foglianus* his vncle by the mothers syde, whoe placed him when he became a striplinge to serve in the warres with *Paulus Vetellin*us, to the ende that beinge well instructed in militarie discipline he might in the ende bee advaunced to some Place of creditt in that vocation. After that *Paule* was dead he followed the warres vnder *Vetellatro*, brother to *Paulus*, and in shorte tyme, (showinge himself wise and well disposed) became one of the cheeffest of the Companie. But callinge to mynde that it was not the parte of a liberall but of a servile mynde to live alwaies vnder the checke of an other mans regimente, he began to practise by the healpe of certeine Citizens, whose abiect myndes coulde better awaye w*i*th bondage then libertie, & w*i*th the ayde of *Vetellin*us to surprise the Cittie of *Firmo*, where he was borne, he wrote therefore *lette*res to his vncle *John Foglianus* to this effect, first he shewed him that havinge lived longe a strainger abroade, he was nowe desirus to vizitt his Contry att home, and to knowe what Patrimony his Father had lefte him, then because in his youthe he travelled to gayne nothinge but hono*ur* to the intente his Citizens mighte see howe well he had bestowed his tyme, he thought best to come thither after the honorablest ma*n*ner he coulde accompanied w*i*th a hundred horss*es* of his frend*es* and servaunt*es*. Lastlie he desired him to take such order that he might be honorably receved of his Citizens, w*h*ich he sayde woulde be asmuch for his glorie, (because he broughte him vpp) as for his owne. His [14] vncle was verie redy to accomplish his request omitting noe circumstance that might increase his creaditt: he caused him honorably to be receved of the Citizens of *Firmo* and lodged him in his owne house, where after he had reposed himself a fewe daies, p*r*eparinge in the meane tyme such thinges as were requisite for the expedic*i*on of his wicked determinac*i*on. Hee caused [15] a solempne feast to be made, wherevnto he invited his vncle *John Foglian* and all the cheeffeste of the Cittie. When the banquet was ended and such beinge removed as served onlie for pleasure,[16] Oliuerottus w*i*th a Counterfett gravitie began to move serious talke touchinge Pope *Alexander* and the power of his Sonne *Valentinus*, and of their [17] doinges; wherevnto when his vncle and the rest were aunsweringe he sodainlie rose vpp sayinge these things are to be resoned of in [f16] a secretter place and therevppon w*i*thdrewe himself to a by chamber whither his vncle and the rest followed him. They [18] were noe sooner sett but certeine Soldiers rushing owte of a secret Place where they were hidden, presentlie slewe both his vncle and all the rest. After w*h*ich slawghter *Oliuerottus* gott on horsbacke accompanied w*i*th his pertakers rann through the Cittie, and in the pallace [19] beseeged the Cheeffest Magestrate. The inhabitantes beinge striken w*i*th a sodaine feare durst not withstande him, wherevppon he framed a goverment agreeable to his owne lyking whereof he made himself prince, after he had putt to death all such as either were iniured by his detestable facte, or offended with his bluddie proceedinges, he strengthened himself in soe good order both with Civill ordinances and martiall pollecyes, that in the compasse of one yeare after he had gott the Crowne, he lived not onlie safe from all daynger within the Cittie of *Firmo*, but caused alsoe his name to be feared of all his neighbours rownde abowte him. And [20] he had ben as hard to be overcom as *Agathocles* was, yf he had not suffred him self to be entrapped by Duke *Valentinus* att *Senogalia* where the *Vrsines* & *Vetellines* (as yow haue heard) were slaine, and where [21] he himself together with *Vitelloclio* his maister of whom he learned bothe his vertues and vitious quallities, one yeare after the horible slaughter he made att *Firmo* was strangled. Some men may mervaile howe it comes to passe that *Agathocles* or any other such after soe many traiterous and cruell partes could possiblie live in safetie in their Contrie both free from the invasions of owtward Enemies, and conspiracies of their owne Cittizens, consideringe that others onlie for their Crueltie haue as well in the tyme of peace as warr ben in dainger of the vtter ruyne of their Estates. I thincke this falles owte accordinge as the cruelltie is well or ill handled, it maybe sayde to be well handled (yf wee maye speake well of that which is ill) when one vrged thervnto by necessitie, dothe once in his lyffe committ a crueltie to purchase his owne safetie, meaninge not to continewe in that vayne but convert it rather by all meanes to the benefitt and proffitt [22] of his subiectes, and it maybe thoughte ill handled, when thoughe in the begininge it be not greate, yet in processe of tyme it rather increase then deminish, it may soe fall owt by gods providence and mens ayde, that those which practise the first kynde, maye fynde some remedie for their estates as *Agathocles* did, but as for the other it is impossible they should continewe.

Wherefore he that will clymbe by this meane to a principality must be sure to obserue this, that he practise all his crueltie att once and leaue noe occasion to vse it afterwarde, the onlie desistinge from that cruell severitie, will promise those that remayne a certeine securitie, and showinge him self liberall in bestowinge benefittes, he shall fynde them loyall in all dutifull obedience. But yf either his owne foolish feare or other mens evill councell, doe cause him to practise it often, he shall bringe himself into that straighte, that alwaies [23] he shalbe driven to stande as it were with his sworde drawen, and never be hable to settle a good fowndacion of his raigne in the heartes of his subiectes, whoe in tyme to com can hope for noe safty, having in tyme past ben plauged with such continewall iniuries. Wherefore iniuries are to be offered all at a clappe, and that but once, that beinge seldom fealt they maybe the sooner forgotten. But benefites contrariwise muste be bestowed by little and little one after an other, that beinge often practised they may the freshlier be remembered. Aboue all thinges a Prince ought to settle his coorse of lyffe emonge his subiectes vpon such firme growndes, that noe fortune good or badd cause him to stagger; for yf he be once broughte [24] to adversitie it is noe tyme to be cruell, and courtesy will stande him in as little steede, for they will thincke it doonn againste his will, and soe not worthy god a mercie.

Of Ciuill Principalities.   *Cap:* 9.

Bᵁᵀ ᴺᴼᵂᴱ to come to the other p*ar*te of my division, that
is when one private Citizen by noe wicked meanes nor
intollerable violence, but onlie by *th*e favo*ur* and furtheraunce of the rest, becomes Prince of his Contrie w*hich* maybe
termed (a *Civill principalitie*) to the atteyninge whereof,
neither vertue alone, nor fortune is necessarie, but rather a
fortunate subtillitie. This[1] kynde of principalitie is gotten
either by favo*ur* of the Co*m*munaltie or frendshipp of the
nobilite. Ffor in everie Cittie those twoe sortes are co*m*monlie
of contrarie factions, because the co*m*mon people woulde
not by their will*es* be co*m*maunded, much lesse oppressed by
the noble men, and the nobilitie seeke nothinge soe much as
to be hable to co*m*maunde and opresse them, of these contrary desires springe one of these three event*es*, either a prince
or libertie, or vnbridled licentiousnes. A prince is chosen
either by the co*m*mon people, or the nobility, as either of
them haue occasion to redresse their wronges. Ffor when the
nobility see that they[2] are not hable to restraine the owtrage
of the people, they streight putt all the authoritie into one
mans hand*es*, whom they choose emonge themselues, and
make him kinge, that vnder coollo*ur* of his soveraignty they
may better shaddowe their owne seu*er*ity. [f17]

The people likewise when they see noe meane to bridle
the loftye attemptes of the nobilite make choyce of one of
their owne Companie whom theye rayse to the dignitie of a
prince hopinge to be shaddowed vnder the covert of his
winges. He that is advanced by the helpe of the Nobillitie[3]
shall fynde more adoe to mainteine his authoritie, then he
that comes to it by the consente of the Co*m*mon people, be-

cause he shall haue manie abowte him that will thincke themselues his equall*es*, and therefore he shall not be hable either
to followe his owne will as he woulde, or co*m*maunde them
.as he shoulde, but he that is made Prince by the favo*ur* of
the people shall haue the swoorde in his owne hande, and
shall fynde either fewe or none abowte him that will not be
willinge to obey.[4] Besydes this, Noble mens courtesie in such a
case cann never be requited accordinge to their expectation,
nor lightlie w*i*thowt the iniurie and losse of other men, but
the co*m*mon people may easilie be satisfied, for the drifte
and purpose of the Co*m*minalltie in this poynte is honester
then that of the nobillitie, the one sorte indeavoringe howe to
oppresse the other sekinge meanes not to be overtrodden. To
this maybe added that a prince erected by the noble men,
can promise himself noe securitie, yf the people resist him,
because they are manie, but thoughe the nobillitie storme
he[5] neede not care for that they are fewe, the verie woorst
inconvenience that can betide a prince by the malice of the
people, is to be forsaken and neglected of them, but yf the
noblemen be incenst against him, they will not onlie forsake him, but attempte some mischeef against his person,
for they havinge a farther[6] reason & deeper forecaste prevente the woorst to make their owne estate sure, and enter
alliaunce w*i*th him whom they hope shalbe conquero*ur*. Beside[7] all this a prince is constrayned to live continuallie w*i*th
the self same people, but not w*i*th these same noble men, for
them he maye advaunce and depresse, rayse vpp and plucke
downe att his pleasure.

But to discusse this poynte the better, wee must consider
twoe wayes of the nobillitie, whether in the wholle coorse
of their proceeding*es* they depende onlie vppon the fortune
of the prince or noe, yf they doe, and be noe extortioners,
they are well woorthie both to be loved and honored, yf they

will not tye them selues to his good lucke, then eyther they doe it for feare, proceedinge of a timerous mynde, and then the Prince maye safelie vse them for his owne advantage (speciallie yf they be wise in Councell) for while thinges succede well they will doe him hono*ur*, and yf fortune frowne they are not to be feared: or el*les* they refuse it for mallice or some ambitious conceipt, w*hi*ch shewes that they haue more regarde of their owne estates thenn their Princes safetie, of these sorte a prince oughte to take good heede, and reckon them in the noombre of his professed Enemies, for lett him be sure (yf oportunity be offerred) they will doe their best to hoyse him owt of his seate.

He that is raysed to the state of a prince by the favo*ur* of the People, hath greate reason to indeavo*ur* to continewe their frendshipp and good likinge, w*hi*ch seeinge they seeke nothinge but that they be not oppressed, is a thinge easilie to be doon, but he that hath gotten the Crowne againste the goodwill*es* of the people, by the ayde of the noble men, aboue all thing*es* ought to currye favo*ur* w*i*th the co*mm*u-naltie, and gett they*r* good liking*es*, w*hi*ch is a matter of noe greate difficultie, yf he take vppon him to protecte and defende them; for when they shall see themselues releeved and well delte w*i*thall att his hand*es*, of whom they looked for nothinge but iniurye and wronge, they wilbe as ready to obey his proceeding*es*, as yf by their meanes he had benn invested in the kingdome. A prince by soondry wayes may wyn the Peoples heart*es*,[8] w*hi*ch because they chaynge accordinge to the diversitie of accident*es*, cannot be compre-hended w*i*thin the compasse of anie certeine rule, I will there-fore omytt them, and onlie sett downe this for a principle, that aboue all thing*es* it is necessarie for a prince to haue the goodwill of the people, otherwise in adversitie he shall fynde noe certeine refuge.

Nabides kinge of *Lacedemon* beseeged by the power of all *the* Princes of *Greece*, and assaulted by a puissante armye of the *Romans*, was hable by the ayde of his owne people to resist their force, and defende his contrie from their threates, and himself from their malice. In the beginninge of these trowbles he was driven to banishe and make awaye a fewe greate men whom he mistrusted, whereby he prevented their spyghte, and [f18] provided sufficientlie for his owne safetie: which he coulde never haue broughte to passe, yf the Communalty had been incenced against him. He that againste this my opinion will obiect the olde proverbe (*He buylds his house on slyme that dependes on the peoples fauour;*) deceaveth himself, for this sayinge takes place only when a private Cittizen will make him self stronge by the multitude, thinckinge by their ayde to make head againste the magestrates, or owtbandy his Enemyes, in such case he shall fynde himself often deceaved, as it happened att *Roome* to the *Gracchi*, and att *Florence* to *George Scalo*. But [9] yf a prince in possession doe take this coorse that hath power to commaunde, and is a man of coorrage, and will not be amazed in adversitie, and lacketh neither meanes nor mynde to holde the multitude vnder his obeysance, he shall both perceve & confesse that the favour of the people is the surest fowndacion that he can laye for the Continewaunce of his estate.

These kyndes of principalities fall often to vtter ruyne and deceaye,[10] when from this civill kynde of authoritie they be raysed to a more absolute manner of sovereinty. Ffor such provinces doe ether governe by themselues, or by their officers; the laste kynde of governmente is more subiect to daynger, and puttes their state in greater hazard, for they are driven to depende vppon the fayth and pleasure of such as rule vnder them. Whoe when any trowbles doe arise, may

easilie defeate them of their kingdomes, either by open
resistance or privy conspiracies. The prince in such a tyme
of tumulte cannot possiblie vse his absolute authoritie to
redresse these wronges, for the citizens which are invred
to the obedience of their magestrates in such trowblesom
tymes will sticke to them lyke burres. Soe that the prince
(wrapped in these perplexitys) shall wante those whom he
may boldlie trust, and not be hable to warraunte himself of
their frendship in his trowble, that shewed him fayrest
faces when all thinges were quiett: for when the Cittizens
haue neede of a kinge, then everie man runnes to offer his
service, every one makes haste to promise his fidelitie, everie
man will dye for him when there is noe daynger, and
defende his cause when he is not oppressed. But when the
prince hath neede of the Cittizens, when trowbles doe rise,[11]
and the perill is iminente, the case will soone be altered,
they will flynch from their promises, and leave him in the
midste of the briers. The[12] experience of this is daingerus,
because the triall thereof will fall owte but once, therefore
a wise and prudente Prince ought soe to provide, that
his Cittizens[13] be alwaies vnder the checke of his owne
government, and haue neede of his helpe, soe shall he keape
them in subiection and himself in safety.

How the force and strength of a principalitie maybe knowen.   Cap: 10.

HE THAT will rightlie examine the strength & force of a
Principality must first consider whether the prince be
of sufficient power himself to mainteine the right he hath,
and redresse[1] the wronges that shalbe offerred him, or
shalbe compelled in such cases to craue the ayde of others,

and flye to them for succour. And to make this more playne, I accompt those princes of sufficient hability to vpholde their owne estates, that either by the nombre of men or store of treasure are hable to levye a competent Armye to geeue battell to any that will offer them iniury. And these contrariwise to neede the ayde and assistaunce of others that Dare not shewe their faces in the fyelde, but are driven to lurke in their stronge holdes and defende themselues within the walles of their citties.

Of the first sorte wee haue entreated already, and will speake more hereafter as occasion shall serve, of the other there is little to be sayde but onlie this to advise all princes that they fortify and strengthen their greate ² cittyes and take noe care for the rest of their territories; for the Prince *that* hath hys cheeffe Cittie well fortified and can in the wholle coorse of his actions beare him self with that courtesy and magestie towardes his subiectes, that wee haue prescribed before; shall not lightlie fynde an enemy soe desperate that will adventure to disturbe his state, or sett himself in armes against him. Ffor wise men will alwaies be loathe to take in hande those enterprises that are dangerouse to attempte, and hard to accomplishe. And surelie he shall fynde a matter of noe small difficultie [f19] that ventures to Invade the contrie, or disquiett the governmente of a prince that hath his Cittie well fenced, and his people well affected towardes him. The Citties of *Germanye* are freest of all other,³ yet haue they small possessions withowt their walles, they obey the Emperour ⁴ when they liste, and neither feare him nor anie other potentate that borders vppon them, for they are soe well provided that everie man perceaues it to be a matter of infinite dainger and noe lesse difficultie to make a Conquest of them, everie cittie beinge compassed with deepe and broade dyches, and environed with strong and highe walles,

havinge besides sufficient Artillerie, armours, and alwayes in
their storehouses provision before hande of Corne, wyne,
and woodd, to serve for one wholle yeare, and because the
multitude maybe keapte withowt the charge of the Commonwealthe, they imploy them in such woorkes as serve both
for the mayntenaunce of the Citty, and sustenaunce of themselues, feates of armes and the knowledge thereof they haue
in greate reputacion, and to continewe and increase the same
they have many lawes, and many good orders. These
thinges considered, it is not likelie that a prince which hath
a stronge Cittie, and loving subiectes, shoulde be assayled
by anie man, or yf anie woulde be soe madde to offer him
that wronge, he shoulde paye the price of his owne follie
and retyre with shame enoughe, for all worldlie affaires are
naturallie accompanied with such variablenes and inconstancie, that it is in a maner ympossible that one with an armie
shoulde continewe a wholle seege together.

Yf anie man will obiect that when the people shall see
their goodes and possessions in the contrie burnte,[5] and themselues shootte vpp [6] within the walles of their cittie, that then
they wax wearie of the longe seige and havinge respect to
their owne proffitt will quicklie forgett their dutie to their
prince. I aunsweare that a wise and valiaunte prince may by
good discreasion soone remove these [7] dowbtes, partlie by
puttinge them in hope that theise violent trowbles cannot
longe endure, partlie by terrifiinge them with the reporte
of the crueltie, and alsoe by practisinge with them that the
people accompte most hardie, to geeue oute that the dainger
is not greate.[8] Besides this the Enimie (as the coorse of warr
requirethe) must even att his first arivall att the beginninge
of the seige committ the owtrages in burninge and wasteinge
spoylinge and defacinge their goodes and possessions when
the peoples Chollour is att the hottest, and their myndes

readiest to resist, and therefore the prince [9] hath lesse cause to dowbte for the harme is doon err their anger be past, and the hurte receaved before they haue leasure to bethincke them of the mischeef. Then when they see that yealding cannot redresse their wronges, nor geeving over recover their losses, they will sticke close to their Prince, and thincke them selues bownde soe to doe, for asmuch as they haue seene their fearmes burned, and their good*es* spoyled for his sake and in his defence. Ffor such is the nature of men, that they accompte them selues as much bownde to those whom they haue benefited, as to those of whom they haue receaved pleasures. Wherefore yf yow looke into the depthe of this matter yow shall fynde it an easie matter for a prince to keepe the myndes of his cittizens and subiect*es* both before, and after the seige [10] constante, and steedfast. Provided alwaies that they wante noe victuall*es* to expell hunger, nor munition to repell their Enemyes.

*Of the principalities or iurisdictions that Bui-
shops & clergy men haue.*[1]   *Cap:* 11.

Nowe there remayneth onlie that wee speake somwhat of ecclesiasticall Principalities the difficulties whereof consiste onlie in the gettinge. To promote men to these Estates,[2] there is necessarilie required either vertue or fortune, but neither of them is required to vpholde them in their dignitie, for they are mainteyned by certeine anciente orders of *Religion,* which of themselues are of that force and efficacie, that howe soever their governo*urs* live or behaue themselues [3] they are sufficientlie hable to defende them in their estates & principalities.[4] These onlie men of all other haue principalities and defende them not, haue subiect*es,* whom

they maye co*m*maunde, and haue noe care howe they are
governed, their provinces lye open, and yet noe man invad*es*
them, their people are neglected, yet raise they noe rebellion,
naye they are soe farr from slydinge from their allegeau*n*ce,
that it comes not in their myndes to thincke of any innovation
neither (yf they thought it) coulde [f20] they bringe
it to passe, these principalities therefore are onlie [5] secure
and happy, but because they be governed by a devyne spirite,
and iudgmente wherevnto mans wisdom canno͟t reache,
I will discoorse of them noe farther: [6] for seinge godd himself doth protect and vpholde them, it were greate arrogancie
and to bolde a parte of me to search to deeplie into his
secrett*es*. Yet [7] yf any man will aske me howe the pope hath
enlarged soe greatlie his temporall dominions, seinge that
before the tyme of *Alexander* the vj[th] there was [8] never a
Duke in all *Italie*, and not soe onlie but never a Lorde nor
pettie Barron that had anie authoritie or iurisdiction,[9] that
had soe little as he in temporalties, whereas nowe he is growne
to that greatnes that he was hable to drive soe mightie [10] a
prince as the *French* kinge owte of *Italie*, and deface the
authoritie of the *Venetians*, w*h*ich thoughe it be sufficientlie
knowen, yet I thincke it will not be [11] lost labo*ur* somewhat
to revive [12] the memorie thereof. Before the kinge of
Fraunce sett foote in *Italye*, the Pope, the Venetians, the
kinge of *Naples*, and the Duke of *Millaine* and *Florence*, had
the wholle cuntrye vnder their subiection.

The [13] Potentates first should haue had especiall care
that noe straynger w*i*th force of Armes should haue passed
into Italie, and then that noe one w*i*thin themselues should
attempte to inlarge his Dominions, those that were to be
suspected to enterprise either of these twoe mischeeff*es*
were the pope, and the *Venetians*. Yf the *Venetians* had the
onlie agremente of the rest in ioyninge their forces as they

did once in the defence of *Ferrara*, it had ben sufficient to
bridle their ambition and to withholde the pope from attemptinge the lyke. The noble men of *Roome* did suffise,
whoe beinge devided into twoe factions of *Vrsines* and
Columnians,[14] woulde never[15] be without quarrelles and
brawlles, whoe beinge continuallie in armes one againste an
other, before the popes face, must needes[16] weaken his power
and abate his courrage. And althoughe that some man of
deeper iudgmente, and noble coorrage as *Xistus* was, should
happen to be chosen pope, yet coulde neither the favour of
fortune, nor his owne skill in matters of state ridd him of
these inconveniences. The cheeffe cause whereof was the
shortnes of the Popes lives, for all that ever a pope coulde
doe in tenn yeares (which was the longest tyme that any
of them lived) was scarce able to make those that helde
on his syde of equall power with the contrarie faction, much
lesse to roote owte anie one of them, for this was the manner,
yf one pope had almost supprest the power of the *Columnians*, the nexte would be a mortall enemye to the *Vrsines;*
whoe would raise their adversaries owte of the duste, and
doe what he could vtterlie to subverte and overthrowe them,
and their faction. This was the cause why[17] the power of
the pope in temporall matters was of soe small accompte
emonge the princes of *Italie*. After this, rose *Alexander* the
vj[th], whoe of all his predecessors did best shewe what a
pope coulde doe by the helpe of men and monye: he made
Valentinus his sonne the instrument to execute his purpose,
and tooke[18] opportunitie by meanes of the frenchmens cominge into *Italie*, which wee haue before handled more at
large, intreatinge of the deeds of Duke *Valentinus*. And
althoughe the drifte of *Alexander* the vj[t] was not to enlarge
the bowndes of the popes iurisdiction, but to raise his soonne
to the dignitie of a prince, yet soe it fell owte that all that

ever was atchived by Duke *Valentin*us, was after annexed
to the popes dominions, for after his death and his soonns
overthrowe, the succeedinge popes enioyed their Conquest*es*
and were heyres of their laboures. After him succeeded *Julius*
the seconde, whoe fownde the popes dominions woonder-
fullie increased, havinge all the province of *Romania* in subiection, and the noble men of *Roome* almost worne owte, and
their factions of noe force by the oppression of *Alexander*,
he alsoe fownde newe inventions to gather monie w*h*ich
before *Alexanders* tyme were never heard of, all w*h*ich he
not onlie followed, but increast and augmented them w*i*th
greate care and dilligence. Ditermininge to ioyne *Bolonia*
to his dominion to cutt off the *Venetians*, and to drive the
frenchmen owte of *Italie*, all w*h*ich succeded fortunatelie
accordinge to his devise, and the more to his co*m*mendacion,
for that in all his doinges he soughte not the benefitte of anie
private person, but onlie the enlarginge of the kingdom of the ·
pope. He [19] continewed the factions of the *Vrsines*, and
Columnians, in that state where he fownde them, and althoughe there were some emonge them that would gladlie
haue ben authors and ringleaders of newe striff*es* and seditions, yet twoe thing*es* kepte them still vnder obedience;
[f21] one was the greatnes that the churche was sproonge
vnto, w*h*ich amazed them, the other that they had none of
their kinred or alliaunce in the wholle College of *Cardinalls*
w*h*ich were woonte to be the verie autho*u*rs of the striff*es*
and contention emonge them, for these factions will never
haue ende soe longe as there be Cardinall*es* to backe them.
It is they onlie that doe breede in *Rome* and in other places
p*a*rtaking*es*, and noble men are driven to ayde and defende
them. Soe that the ambition of the prelates doth breede discorde emonge the nobility; nowe [20] hath Pope *Leo* gotten the
popedom, enriched w*i*th all these welthie dominions, of

whom there is greate hope (that yf other haue raysed it to this heighte by force [21] of Armes) he by the integritie of his lyffe, and other infynite vertues, will increase it in power and make it more glorious. *Finis.*

Howe manye kyndes of soldiers there are and of such as are hired. *Cap:* 12.

Havinge runn over this matter [1] concerninge Principalities, which I purposed in the beginninge to discourse of, shewinge partelie the causes of their good or ill successe, and vnfoldinge the meanes and devises that many [2] haue practised to gett and alsoe [3] to keepe them. There remayneth onlie [4] that I shoulde intreate of those [5] thinges in a generalitie, which in such estates seeme ether to offende or defende; [6] it is sayde before that princes above all thinges ought to laye good fowndacions of their highe estates or elles it is impossible that they shoulde continewe. The [7] beste and most assured growndwoorkes that vpholde anie estate or principalitie, whether it be newe or olde, or mixte of both those, [8] are good Lawes and good Armes, but because the effecte of good Lawes is weake when the force of good Armes is wantinge, [9] I will passe over them and speake onlie att this tyme of Armes. The Armes which any prince dothe vse to defende his seate [10] and dominions, are ether his owne, or hyred, or assistantes, or mixed of these kyndes, the mercenarie and assistantes are bothe vnproffitable and daingerouse. The Prince whose state dependes vppon the ayde of hyred soldiers holdes by a weake threed, and shall never be secure, for these mercenarie men are seditious, ambitious, withowte all discipline, withowte all faithe or honestye, stowte and cruell to their frendes, slouthfull & Cowardes emonge theyr

Enemyes, neither fearinge god, nor caringe for men: [11] so
that the state of the prince that hyreth them is noe longer
assured then whille they remayne vnassaulted: in tyme of
peace he shalbe spoyled by them, and in tyme of warr by his
Enemyes: [12] the reson of this is, because they serve not for
loue but for lacke, not for goodwill but for gayne, which
is not of sufficiente force to cause them to venter their lives
in his defence. They loue to receave paye, but not to take
payne, in peace noe men soe greedie of their pencions, nor in
warr non soe readie to run away, alwaies sure to be farthest
of when the prince that hyreth them standes in most neede of
their healpe, which maye easlie be proved, for what elles is
the cause of the present ruyne and overthrowe of *Italye*, but
that they haue soe longe relyed vppon foreyne force,
and putt their affyaunce in the ayde of hyred soldiers,
which in tyme paste stood some in good steede, and shewed
greate prooffe of their valour: but assone as the contrie was
invaded by a mightie force of straingers, they quicklie
shewed what hope might be conceived of such kynde of
men. Which caused *Charles* kinge of *Fraunce* soe easilie to
passe through the conquest of *Italie*. They that alleage *that*
mens offences were cause of these mischeef*es*, [13] saie trulie,
but yet not the offences of them which perhapp*es* they
blame for it, but of such as wee haue made mencion of before.
Which beinge all princes, haue all woorthelie feltt the smarte
thereof. To [14] prove more manifestlie the imperfection and
unluckines of these kynde of Armes, consider this whether
the hyred Captaines be men of great prowes, endued with
excellent vertues or noe. Yf they be thowe canste never committ thy self safelie into their handes, for havinge aspiringe
myndes to increase their owne glorie, they will either oppresse them vnder whose regiment they serue or iniury others
contrarie to thy purpose and expectation, yf they be men of

base myndes and noe currage, they must needes be the cause of thy utter ruyne and overthrowe. Yf anie will obiecte that whoe soever hathe the commaundinge of the fylde is lyke to plaie the same parte, whether he be hyred or noe. I aunsweare that the warres are either taken in hande by a prince or a commonweale: yf by a prince, he oughte to be there [15] in person and to be cheefe [f22] Comaunder himself, yf by a commonweale, they owughte to appoynte for that purpose some of their cheefe Cittizens, amonge whom yf anie be fownde that for vertue or valour aunsweare not their expectacion, he muste streight be [16] removed, yf fitt to supplie the place, they must with good lawes soe bridle his aspiringe thoughtes, that he maye not passe the bowndes [17] of his office and dutie. Experience it self hath taught vs that Princes and common weales with their owne powers haue atchived manie greate enterprises and that mercenarie soldiers haue alwaies hindered and hurte those that hyred them, moreover a commonwealth [18] fenced with the power of their owne men, will hardlier [19] be broughte in subiection to any private Citizen, then that which is defended by the force of hyred straingers. *Rome* and *Lacedemon* vsinge their owne powers continewed manie yeares free from all subiection. The *Suisers* in like maner are a most warlike nation and lived with as greate libertie as anie men. To shewe the nature of hyred soldiers, wee haue an example of the *Carthaginians* whoe in their first warres against the *Romans,* were putt in greate hazard to be overthrowne vtterlie [20] by such mercenarie men as they had hyred for their defence. All their owne Citizens were cheefe captaines of their Armie. The *Thebans* after the deathe of *Epiminondas,* chose *Phillip of Macedon* [21] for generall of their armie, whoe had noe sooner gotten the victorie over their Enemies, but streighte wey broughte them in subiection, and tooke from them their libertie. The *Millanishe* after the deathe of *Phillip* their duke, waged *Frauncis Sforza* [22] against the *Venetians,* whoe after he had overcome his Enemies att *Carouagio,* ioyned frendship with the vanquished, to oppresse his maister that hyred him. *Sforza* his father beinge hyred to serve *Jane Quene of Naples,* forsooke her on the sodaine, soe [23] that for savegarde of her Realme, she was driven to flye for succour to the kynge of *Aragon.*

Yf anie will obiect that the *Venetians,* and *Florentines,* haue both defended longe and greatlie encreased their dominions by this kynde of Armes, and yet hath their Captaines neither abridged their liberties, nor brought them to subiection. I aunsweare that the *Florentines* may thancke [24] their good fortunes which provided better for them, then they did for them selues, for of their Captaines which were stoughte and valiante men, of whom they had anie cause to stande in dowbte, some were not vanquishers, some were crost with other warres, and some were carried awaye with the ambition of other enterprises. Amonge these that had ill successe in their attemptes *John Auentho* was one, whose faithe to the *Florentines* (seinge he was noe conquerour) can hardlie be devined [25] of. But had he gotten the victorie, nonne will denie but they had ben all att his mercie; *Sforza* had alwaies the *Brachians* his adversaries, soe that one of them hindered the other. *Sforza* bent his force against *Lumberdie* and *Brachius* turned his strengthe against the pope, and the kinge of *Naples.* But lett vs come to that which fell owte of late. The *Florentines* did choose *Paule Vitellius* generall of their warres, a man of greate iudgment, whoe beinge att the firste a man of verie base condicion, had gotten a name of verie greate reputacion, yf he had subdued *Pisa* noe man can deeme but that he might haue commaunded [26] the *Florentines;* for yf he had ioyned his force with their adversaries and been [27] hyred of them, the *Florentines* had ben lefte in

noe possibility to escape, or yf he had continuallie kepte them
paye, they muste in the ende of force haue yealded to his
goverment.

He that will looke [28] into the proceedinges of the *Venetians,* shall easilie fynde howe safelie and luckelie they did
beare themselues soe longe as they made warre with an armye
of their owne Nation, which was their manner before they
gaue their myndes to attempte any exployte by lande,[29] then
should yow haue seene the gentlemen and communaltie, in
their armies behave them most valiauntlie, but as soone as
they begann [30] to make warr by lande,[31] they were nothinge
soe forwarde, their coorrage waxed colde, and then they followed the custome and manner of *Italie.* And at the first
when that they did begynn to increase their dominions, there
was noe greate cause whie they shoulde stande in feare of
the power of their Captaines, aswell for that they had not
greatlie enlarged the [32] bowndes of their commonwealthe,
as alsoe for that they themselues for their former vertue and
prowes were had [33] in greate estimation. But [34] when their
Empire once waxed greate they quicklie sawe manifest
prooffe of their errour. And they had chosen *Carmignola* [35]
generall of their Armie, for knowinge him to be a most
valiaunte Captaine, after they had vnder his conducte overthrowen the Duke of Millaine, perceavinge that he waxed
colde in matters of Warr, they were sure [f23] they should
atchive noe more victories vnder his leadinge, yet they coulde
not, nor durst not dismisse him, leaste they shoulde loose that
which they had alreadie woon; wherefore to ridd themselues
from feare, they were constrained to putt him to deathe.[36]
They had after for their generalles [37] *Bartholomewe* of *Bergamo, Robert* of *Sanuerino,* & the Earl of *Petigliano,* and
such others by whose service, they had greater cause to
feare losse, then to hope for gaine, which did well appere

by that w*h*ich happened att *Vayla* where att one iourney
they lost all that had ben gotten with greate labo*ur* in eight
hundred yeares.

Small is the gayne and glorie that comes by the ayde &
force of hyred soldiers and longe looked for er it happen,
but greate is the losse, and calamitie, and falles owte on the
sodaine, and for asmuch as these examples haue brought vs
to speake of *Italie*, w*h*ich contrie longe tyme hath vsed the
ayde and force of these kynde of soldiers, I have thought
good more preciselie to searche the deapthe of that matter,
that when they shall see the originall [38] cause of their cominge
hither and the maner of their pr*o*ceding*es* whille they haue
ben emongste vs, they may alter their counsell*es* and take a
better coorse.

Yow must note that as soone as the empire of the *Romanes*
was translated owte of *Italie* into *Greece*, and that the
clergie [39] more and more begann to intermeddle w*i*th temporall matters, as Italie was devided into soondrie states, manie
of the cheeffe citties did rise [40] in Armes against their noble
men which before by the emperours favour had ruled &
kept them in awe.[41] The clergy thereby to encrease their
estimation in temporall causes, did not sticke to take their
partes, by w*h*ich meanes they broughte Citties vnder their
rule and subiection, soe that the government of all Italie fell
into the handes of the clergie, and certeine Co*m*monwealthes
the one sort beinge preestes, and the other cittiezens, both
altogether vnskilfull and ignoraunte in martiall affaires, they
began to hyre soldiers for monie, the first that gaue creaditt
to these kynde of Warres was *Albericus Comensis* [42] of the
Province of *Romagnia*. Owte of this mans schoole came
Brachius & *Sforza*, whoe in their tyme disposed of all matters
in *Italye* att their pleasures, after them, have succeded all
those that haue co*m*maunded the Armies [43] of Italie and

strooke [44] the stroake in matters of Warr vntill this daie: of all whose glorious Actes and chivalrye this wee see hath ben the evente & issue that *Italie* hath ben overrunn by *Charles*, spoyled by *Lewes*, oprest by *Ferdinando*, and defaced by the *Swisers*, their practise att the first was to take all reputacion from the footmen and to geive it to the horsmen, and this was doon because they havinge noe lande nor possessions, but were driven to live onlie by their swoorde & service, coulde make noe shewe with a fewe footemen, and manie they were not able to bringe; wherefore all their service was on horsbacke, because their captaines with a small nombre of them mighte be more honorablie received, and better enterteyned: they had brought the matter to that passe that in an armie [45] of twentie thowsande men, yow shoulde scarce fynde ij^m footmen. [46] The chef care they [47] had was to ridd them selues and their men from labour and to take awaie all occasions of feare, that there might be noe slaughter emonge [48] them but onlie takinge of prisoners which shoulde be sent home againe withowt ransom, they never gaue assaulte by night to anie Cittie beseiged, nor they of the Cittie att that tyme might offer to come owte againste the Enimies tentes. They [49] entrenched not their campe with dyches nor fortified it with anie rampyre, nor never keapte the fyeldes in the winter seison. All these thinges were permitted and invented of them in their militarie discipline to noe other ende [50] as I haue sayde but to avoyde travell of bodie, and daynger of lyffe, soe by these meanes Italie was brought to slaverie and vtter discreditt.

Of *Armies or strengthe of Soldiers that are termed assistantes, or mixed, or a princes owne.* Cap: 13.

THOSE Armes[1] or strengthe of Soldiers that wee terme assistantes (which are likewise compted verie vnproffit-able) are such as some mighty man att thy request sendes to succour and defende[2] thee. Which not longe synce was putt in practise by Pope *Julius* the seconde, whoe perceavinge the evill[3] successe of his hyred Soldiers thought to prove what he coulde doe by the ayde of some mightie assistante.[4] Hee agreed therefore with *Ferdinando* Kinge of *Spaine* to haue from thence a power of men of armes sente him into *Italye*. This kynde of Armes in their owne nature maybe both good and proffitable, but alwaies most dayngerous to him that shall sende for them, for yf they be vanquished he is overthrowne, and yf he gett the victorie by their meanes, he shall stande [f24] att their mercie. Although the anciente histories are full of these Examples yet I will [not][5] overslipp this Example of Pope *Julius* which is yet fresh in memorie, whoe coulde not possiblie take a woorse course then committ the enterprise of *Ferara* into the handes of strayngers. But his[6] great good fortune by a woonderfull chaunce helped him to escape the iminente daynger which for his indiscreete choyce he had worthelie deserved.

Ffor the armye of his assistantes beinge overthrowne before *Rauenna* by the *Frenchmen*, sodainelie the *Swisers* vn-looked for beyonde all hope, or the expectation of him, or anie man elles, came[7] to his rescue, fought with the van-quishers and putt them to flight,[8] wherebie he escaped the crueltie and prison[9] of his enemyes, & was not forced to stande to the cortesie and pleasure of his Assistantes, havinge gotten the victory by other mens healpe and not by theyrs.[10] The *Florentines* beinge noe martiall men themselues, pro- cured ten thousande Frenchmen to assist them to wynn the citie of *Pysa*, by which devise they incurred greater daynger then ever they were brought into by all the hard happes of their adversse fortune. The Emperour of *Constantinople* to represse certeine of his neighbours that rose in Armes against him, brought ten thousande turkes into *Greece*, which when the warr was ended woulde never departe from thence, and this without dowbte was the beginninge of the servitude which all *Greece* hath suffered ever synce vnder the infidelles. He therefore that meanes not to be a con- querour were best to vse the helpe of these kynde of soldiers, for these are ten tymes[11] more dayngerous then the mer- cenarie men are, and much more redy to doe a mischeeffe, because they are lyncked in one, and all of a companie, and rather inclyned to an other mans commandement then thyne; wheras hyred soldiers should neede longer tyme and greater occasion err they durste attempte to oppresse thee, thoughe by their meanes thou hadest obteyned the victory, for they are not of one bodie but rather of one bande, gathered and hyred owte of soondrie places; to conclude the negligente care of hyred soldiers, and the aspiringe mindes of the assist- antes, their slouthe, and these[12] mens sleightes, are to be feared, wherefore a wise prince shoulde putt noe confidence in either of them, but eschewe both and bend his mynde to haue good soldiers of his owne, with whom he shoulde choose rather to overcom[13] then be Conquerour with others, estem- inge that[14] noe trewe victorie that is gotten by the healpe of other men. I neede not dowbte to bringe in *Valentinus* for an example, whoe enterred into *Romagnia* with a wholle armie of *French* men that were his assistantes, by whose

healpe he tooke *Imolia* & *Furley;* [15] neverthelesse [16] when he
sawe howe little trust might be reposed in them, he lefte them
and enterteigned mercenarie men in whom he thought there
was lesse dainger, he hyred the *Vrsines*, and the *Vitellians*,
but fyndinge by prooffe how dooble vnfaithfull & perilous
they were, he supprest them and levied [17] an army of his owne
contreemen. What diversitie there was betwene the kynde [18]
of Armes, did easilie appere by the difference of the dukes
reputacion in the tyme he vsed the ayde of the *Frenchmen*
his assistantes, and the help of the *Vrsines* and *Vitellians*, [19]
and then when he relyed onlie vppon his owne power and
proper force. For [20] indeede we fynde that then he began to
floorishe and his name to be of greate accompte, when it was
knowen that he had a power of his owne soldiers: and was
lorde and governour of his owne Armie. I woulde not willinglie goe from the examples of *Italie* which chaunced of late,
but that I cannot leaue owte one of whom I haue made
mention before. I meane *Hierom* of *Seracusa*, who (as I
saide) beinge chosen generall of the *Siracusans* armie, [21] did
quicklie perceave the inconveniences that did arise daylie
by the assistantes and hyred soldiers, whose Captaines might
well be compared to these that wee have in *Italie*, but seinge
he coulde not reteyne them with his profitt, nor refuse them
withowt perrill, he caused them all on the sodaine to be putt
to deathe. And [22] ever after refusinge other mens ayde, made
warr with his owne Armies. I remember a notable example
servinge aptlie to this purpose in the olde testamente. When
Dauid offered himself to fight with *Goliath* the Champion
of the *Philistians; Saule*, (the better to encoorrage him) gaue
him his owne Armour which David havinge tryed on his
backe vtterlie refused, sayinge that he was not hable to stirr
nor shifte for himself while all that was abowte him. But
takinge onlie his owne slinge and his swoord he wente to

meete his adversarie. The effect of all that I haue sayde is this, that other mens armes are either soe wyde [f25] they will not hange on thie shoulders, or heavie that they will wearye thee, or straighte that they will wringe thee.[23]

Charles the viij[th] father vnto *Lewes* the xj[th] when by his fortune and prowes he delivered *Fraunce* from the *English-men* thought good to strengthen his contrie with the power of his owne Soldiers, and therefore throughowte all his king-dom ordeyned bandes of horsmen and footemen to be in redines, whose soonne *Lewes* cutte of the band*es* of foote-men and began to enterteyne the *Swisers* in paye,[24] by which oversight (followed by his successors,) the realme as appeeres att this daye is brought into soe great trowbles and dayngers, for by puttinge the *Swysers* into this reputac*i*on, they im-payred the creaditt of their owne contriemen. Ffootmen they had none of their owne, and their horsmen were bownde to repose their trust in a companie of strayngers, and thus being accustomed to fyghte emongst the *Swisers*, they thincke they can never doe anie woorthy exployte withowte them. The armes and power therefore of the *Frenche*[25] are mixed, of their owne and hyred soldiers, which strengthes ioyned in one are farr better then those which consist onlie of mercen-arie men or assistantes, and much woorse then those armyes that princ*es* haue of their owne naturall Subiect*es* which is proved sufficientlie alreadie, and sure the power of *Fraunce* had ben invinsible, yf the institutions and orders sett downe for militarie affayres by *Charles* had ben maynteyned and encreased by his Successors, but such is the shallownes of mens iudgment*es* that they take matters in hand wherein, because there is some apparau*n*ce and shewe of goodnes, and happie successe, they never perceive (as I sayde before of the feaver *Hectica*) where the poyson and inconvenience lurk-eth,[26] he deserves not the name of a wise and discreete prince, that cannot foresee mischeeff*es* [27] before they happen, and fewe have the guyfte wiselie to prevente them.

Now yf the first cause be sought owte [28] of the ruyne of the Romane Empyre it wilbe fownde that the hyringe of the *Goathes*, was the vearie grownde and roote thereof, for then began the force and strength [29] of the *Romane* Empire to de-caye, and the vertue and prowesse of the auncient *Romanes* was attributed and geeven to the barbarous [30] *Goathes*.

Therefore this is my conclusion that noe principalitie that wanteth proper Armes and power of soldiers w*i*thin it self canbe accompted safe and free from dainger, but lackinge the true meanes to defende it from wronge, must needes bee sub-iect to the inconstancy of fortune, and the wisest men haue alwayes ben of this opinion and iudgmente, that there is nothinge soe vayne, nothinge soe vncertaine, or of soe little momente, as to brage of a power that is not our owne, but other mens; and I call those Armes a prince his [31] owne, w*h*ich consist onlie of his subiect*es*, Cittizens and such as live vnder his obeysau*n*ce, all the rest I accompte either hyred or assistantes. [32] But nowe howe to order and dispose of our owne power and armes, shall not seeme hard, yf we observe and marke the govermente and disciplyne that those of whom wee haue made mencion before, as also that w*h*ich Phillip father to *Alexander* the greate, and manie other com-monwelthes haue vsed in their Camps wherevnto I referr the Reader.

How the prince oughte to be adicted to the knowl-
edge of martiall affayres. *Cap:* 14.

A PRINCE should haue noe other thoughtes [1] in his mynde,
noe other care in his heade, nor exercise his witt abowte
anie other knowledge, but of warr, and the orders and discipline thereof, for this is the onlie skill that belonges to a
prince, and is of that force and efficacie, not onlie to defende
those that come to their [2] kingdomes by inheritau*n*ce and lini-
all discente, but alsoe to rayse private men from their simple
degrees, to that soveraigne dignities: on the other syde it is
evidente that princes w*h*ich rather take pleasure [3] to passe
their tymes delicately, then paynes to practise armes dili-
gentlie, haue lost theyr principalityes, and been deprived of
their glorie: ffor as the p*r*ofession [4] of militarie dissipline was
the first cause of raysinge them to this [5] hono*ur*, soe [6] the
neglectinge thereof, is the cheeffe meanes of their overthrowe and disgrace. *Frauncis Sforza* beinge skilfull in
Armes, of a private man became Duke of *Millaine*, whose
soonnes because they coulde not awaye w*i*th the trowbles
and paynes of warres,[7] of princes became private men; for
besydes other inconveniences that accompanie him that is
not geeven to Armes, this is one speciall thinge, that [f26]
it bringeth him into contempte, w*h*ich amonge all other is the
cheeffe blott aswell to the glorie, as to the safetie of a prince;
and therefore (as I will declare hereafter) w*i*th greate care
and dilligence to be alwaye eschewed: for there canbe noe
agreemente betwene the armed & vnarmed: reason it self not
sufferinge that valiante men shoulde bee subiecte to effeminate persons, or an vnarmed maister to be safe emonge armed
Servauntes. For [8] howe is it possible they shoulde agree, when

in the one sorte there is a generall contempte, and in the other
a continuall suspition. Therefore a prince that is vnskilfull in
Armes can never bee of any reputacion emonge his soldiers,
nor committ himself into their handes. Wherefore he shoulde
never remove his thoughtes from the studie of martiall affayres, and exercise himself more intentivelie therein in the
tyme of peace then war, which he may doe twoe wayes,
either by practise [9] or speculation. Touchinge practise, he
shoulde not only keepe his soldiers and men of Armes in
order and exersise, but alsoe geeue his owne mynde to hunt-
inge, that he maye invre his bodie to labour and travell, and
learne to know the nature and Cituation of diverse places,
markinge the heigthe of the mountaines, the openinge of the
valleys, to admitt enteraunce, and howe the playnes lye, by
this meanes alsoe he shall knowe the coorse of the rivers, their
depthes and passages, the nature of the marishe growndes,
and divers other thinges, in the searche whereof he shoulde
be bothe carefull and dilligente, for the knowledge therof
bringes a dubble commoditie, the one is, that havinge taken
the vewe of his owne contrie, he knoweth better howe to
provide for the defence thereof. The other, that by the skill
and iudgmente he hath in his owne, he may geeue the better
ayme in the discoveringe of an other; [10] for the mountaines,
the valleys, the playnes, and levelles, the fludes, and the
marishes that are in *Tuscan*, haue a resemblaunce and lyknes
to those of other contries, soe that by the survey of one, he
may haue a good guesse att the rest. The Prince that wantethe
iudgment in these matters, lacketh the best propertie belong-
inge to a good Captaine, for thereby dothe he learne to fynde
owte his coonninge to choose his grownde, to conduct his
Armye, to pytch his ffeelde, and to beseige Citties or townes,
to his best advantage. [11] Amonge other commendacions that
writers attribute to *Philopomenon* [12] Prince of the *Achaians*,

this was one that in tyme of peace his thoughtes were alwaies in the warres, and walkinge in the *Fieldes* with his frendes he woulde often staie and reason with them in this sorte. Yf our Enemies were uppon yonder hill and wee here with our Armie, I pray yow whether of vs had the Vantage? by what meanes (keepinge our selues in our ranckes) might we best charge them, how should wee safelie retire yf wee had neede, or speedelie followe them yf they fledd. And [13] soe propowndinge vnto them all cases & casualties that might happen in an armie, he would heare their opinions and declare his owne, and confirme that with resons and soe revolving continewallie these dowbtes in his mynde he soe encreased his knowledge in matters of warr, that leading his armie there coulde happen noe stratagem so subtill, noe accident soe strainge, but he had a present remedie to avoyde the inconvenience thereof. Nowe conserninge speculation wherein the labour of the mynde is onlie required, a prince ought to spende some tyme in readinge of histories,[14] thereby to looke [15] into the woorthy deedes of excellente men, and obserue what councell [16] they followed in the coorse of their warres, notinge both the causes of victorie and losse, that he may followe the proffitt of the one, and fly [17] the perrill of the other: takinge that order with him self that manie notable men have doon before, to conforme [18] all his actions to the imitacion of some speciall man whom he desires to be lyke, and followe him in all poyntes, soe neere as he cann; soe it is reported that *Alexander* the greate imitated *Achilles*, *Cæsar*, *Alexander* and *Sipio*, *Cyrus*, and he that will reade the lyffe of *Cyrus* in *Xenophon* shall easilie see what proffitt, naye what glorie, *Sypio* gayned by imitatinge soe woorthie a man, and alsoe howe nere he conformed himself to that continencie, that affabilitie,[19] that courtesie and liberalitie that *Xenophon* describes to haue ben [20] in *Cyrus*. A wise prince ought both to practise and obserue these preceptes,[21] and not to passe his daies idlely or wantonlie in tyme of peace, but then speciallie to haue these thing*es* in regarde and price that (yf fortune frowne) maye serve for his safetie and defence. [f27] [22]

Of those thinges which cause men and especiallie princes to be either praised or blamed. Cap: 15.

NOWE we are to examine the matter howe a prince should behaue himself, and what coorse of lyffe he shoulde take and [1] leade emonge his people and frendes that are his Subiect*es*, and for asmuch as I knowe many haue written of this Argument, I feare they will accompte me arrogau*n*te to discoorse of the same matter, especiallie, yf I sett downe cleane contrarie maximes to those they haue prescribed. But seeinge my purpose is to publishe such [2] rulles as shall yeald proffitt to the readers, yf it be rightlie vnderstoodd: I thought it most conveniente to followe the substance not the shaddowe, the truth by imitation and not the counterfeit by imagination,[3] for manie in their writing*es* haue fayned co*m*mon wealthes and principalities, that were never seene by others, nor heard of but by themselues, nor are not indeede any where to be fownde; and soe greate is the difference betwene the lyves [4] wee doe leade, and the lives wee shoulde leade: that he w*h*ich respectes not what is doon, but studies onlie to learne that w*h*ich shoulde be doon, is liker [5] by his knowledge to purchase his owne subvertion, then by his co*n*ninge to provide for his safetie; [6] for he that in everie respect will need*es* be a good man cannot choose but be overthrow*n*e emonge soe many that are ill. It is necessarie therefore for a prince, yf he have regarde to his owne

securitie,[7] to knowe howe to be good and badd, and vse
both as the occasion[8] of his accidentes, and necessitie of
his causes shall require. Wherefore to omitt these[9] thing*es*
w*h*ich some fayne to be in a prince by imagination, and to
sett downe that w*h*ich is fownde to be trewe by experience:
I saye, that all men (for I speake generallie) and specially
Princes, (for their ma*n*ners are best marked because they are
placed in highest roomes) are noted for some of these qualities, one is thought liberall and bountifull, an other covetous
and miserable, one geeves freelie of his owne, an other
extortes greedelie from other men, some are reputed cruell,
some covetous, some carelesse of their promise, some constante of their woordes,[10] some effeminate and dasterdes,
other valiant and hardie, manie lowlie and gentle, manie
prowde and churlishe, manie lacivious[11] and wanton, and
manie continente and chaste,[12] some are honored for their
faythe, and some hated for their frawde, manie are compted
asture[13] and currishe[14] in their behavio*ur*, and manie verie
affable and kynde, manie graue and severe, and manie lighte
and dissolute, manie godlie and manie gracelesse, etc.[15] I
knowe all the worlde will confesse that it weere an excellente
co*m*mendac*i*on, for a prince to be indued w*i*th all these good
and co*m*mendable quallities[16] that I haue recited, but seeinge
that noe man can possiblie have them nor by reason of the
weaknes of our frayle nature dulie observe them, it behooves
a prince to vse that discretion whereby he maye avoyde the
infamie especiallie of such vices as maye weken his power, or
hazarde the losse of his principalitie, he shoulde alsoe indeavo*ur* to shunn the rest thoughe they threaten noe such
daynger, but yf he coulde not, he might lett them passe w*i*th
lyght regarde, neither must he be scripulous to straine cour-
tesies to incurr the infamie of such vices as preserve the safetie
of his owne estate, for yf matters be weyed in indifferent bal-

lances, and considered of rightlie as they are indeede, yow shall finde that by practisinge of some thinges that carrie the face and shewe of vertue yow shall purchase your owne ruyne and overthrowe, and that by followinge some other that att the first sight seme vitious, yow shall finde most sure defence for your owne safetie and quietnesse.

Of Liberalitie and sparing.   *Cap:* 16.

TO BEGINN with the first of those quallities that were spoken of before, I cannot denye but that it were to be wished that a prince might be accompted liberall, notwith-standinge to be soe free in his liberalitie that his subiectes shoulde haue cause to feare his lavishinge, is verie daunger-ous. The liberalitie that is doon to anie man after a vertuous sorte, as it ought to be, must not appere to the worlde and then it will not acquite the gever from the suspicion of covetousnes, wherefore to be reputed liberall[1] of the multi-tude, a man must omitt noe kynde of lavishinge in soe much that a prince that is soe geeven, cannot choose but waste his wealthe, and consume his treasure, and shalbe driven in the ende, (yf he will continewe the reputacion of his bownti-fullnes) to oppresse and overburthen his [f28] subiectes, and exacte parte of their livinge to mayntaine the pompe of his owne liberalitie, devisinge all meanes in his heade howe to gett monie into his handes.[2] By these practises shall he becom odious to his subiectes, and beinge once poore, had in noe reputacion of anie man, for havinge hurte manie with his lavishinge, and healped fewe with his liberalitie he shalbe subiecte to a thowsand inconveniences, and in daynger of destruction whensoever anie occasion of trowble is raysed; which when he shall perceve and indeavour to take an other coorse, he shall presentlie gayne himself the name of a miserable and covetous prince. Therefore seinge liberalitie bring*es* losse, and bowntie breed*es* beggerie, a wise prince neede not care greatlie [3] to be accompted thrifftie [4] or covetous. Ffor in processe of tyme when it shall appeere that by his sparinge he hath maynteyned himself vppon his owne revenewe & encreased his treasure, that he is hable to defend himself agaynst his Enemyes, and enterprise matters of greate consequence [5] withowt charginge his Subiectes with taskes and Subsedies, then I saye he shalbe compted more magnificente and bowntifull then the other, for he shalbe thoughte liberall of all those from whom he hath taken nothinge w*h*ich are almost infinite, and be estemed sparinge onlie of them to whom he hath geeven nothinge w*h*ich are but a fewe: In our age we haue seene nothinge doon woorthie [6] co*m*mendac*i*on, but of those w*h*ich haue ben [7] accompted verie covetouse, the rest are worne quite owte of memorie. *Julius* the seconde after that by the opinion of his liberalitie he had obteyned the dignitie of the popedom: he never sought to continewe the glorie of that vayne tytle, but by his sparing and thrifte [8] he was hable vppon his owne charge to make war against the *French King,* and passe throughe manie trowbles, and yet never charged his subiectes, either w*i*th extraordinarie tribute or custome, but by his longe sparinge in tyme of peace gott sufficiente to defraye his charge [9] in all his Warres. The kinge of *Spayne* that nowe is, had never compassed so manie woorthie enterprises, nor atchived soe manie greate victories, yf he had ben desirous to haue ben accompted liberall. Therefore a prince that will not oppresse his subiectes, and yet be hable to mayntaine his estate, and defende his righte, that will not runn himself into povertie and contempte of his people, and yet shame [10] the nature of a tyrante and an extortioner, muste esteeme it lighte to be compted covetous, for this is a vyce that never hynders the quiett raigne of a prince. Yf any will obiecte that *Julius Cæsar* gott his Empire by his liberalitie,[11] and that manie other were raysed to the highest typp of hono*ur* because they were bowntifull. I aunsweare that thow arte either a prince alreadie, or ell*es* aspiring to that dignitie, in the first case thy liberalitie will greatlie hynder thee, in the other greatlie healpe thee.

Cæsar was in the nombre of those that aspired to the *Romayne Empire*, but havinge gotten it, yf he had lived, and had not ben more moderate in his Expenses he woulde have consumed the wholle treasure, and brought the Empire to vtter ruyne & decaye; yf anie will replye againe that manie Princes haue managed great affayres, and with their Armies atchived manie valiante actes, w*h*ich notw*i*thstandinge haue ben lavishe in their guyft*es*, and liberall in their Expences. I aunsweare that a prince spendes vppon his owne charge, or vppon other mens coste. Yf on his owne, he must not be[12] lavishe, yf on other mens he maybe liberall, and never spare to cutt large measure owte of other mens clothe. A prince that leades an armie vppon the enterteinmente of spoyles and sackinge*s*, must needes in those thing*es* be francke, or elles his soldiers will never followe him. For[13] it is greate reason he shoulde be liberall of that w*h*ich is non of his owne, nor his Subiecte*s*. Soe was *Cyrus*, *Cæsar*, and *Alexander;* and take this by the waye, thow shallt not diminishe thie reputac*i*on one iott by that[14] thowe takest from other men, but rather encrease itt. But the cheeffest hurte that can growe to thee is by consuminge that w*h*ich is thine owne; for there is nothinge that doth soe soone decaye as liberalitie. In[15] vsinge whereof, thowe doste waste the meanes to vse it, and soe bringst thy self either to beggerie, or contempte of thye subiecte*s*: or to avoyde that mischeef, doest oppresse & overburthen them, and soe incurr their hate. The cheefest thing*es* that a prince ought to avoyde, is, that he bringe not [f29] himselfe either into Contempte or hatred of his people, into both w*hi*ch mischeeff*es* liberalitie will quicklie drawe him.

Therefore it is much better for a prince to be reputed covetous w*hi*ch bring*es*[16] an infamie w*i*thowte hatred, then by strivinge to be acompted liberall fall flatt to extortion, w*hi*ch breedes a slander w*i*th continewall malice.

Of crueltie and gentlenes, and whether it be better to be loued or Feared. Cap: 17.

Nowe to proceede to other of those quallities w*hi*ch before wee mencioned, it were to be wished that everie Prince shoulde rather desyre to be accompted gentle then cruell. Neverthelesse greate Judgm*ent* is to be had that he abuse not the myldenes. *Valentin*us was reputed pytielesse, yet his crueltie reduced[1] all the province of *Romagnia* into good order, establishinge peace and safetie by austerenes, w*hi*ch beinge by wisdom weighed, he shalbe thoughte lesse rigorous then the *Florentynes*, whoe suffered the Cittie of *Pistoia* to be destroyed whilst they thought to shvnn the name of crueltie. Let therefore a prince esteeme yt[2] lighte to be accompted cruell soe as he maye haue his subiect*es* in fayth by feare. For[3] he shalbe thought more gentle by shewinge a fewe examples of severitie, then they w*hi*ch through foolishe pyttie nowrishe disorders, owte of w*hi*ch springe murthers and[4] mischeefes, for these riott*es* trowble the wholle multitudes.[5] Whereas the prince his rigour onlie concerneth some principall or perticuler men. But emonge all other princes, it is impossible for him to avoyde the name of cruell, that is latelie advanced to his governmente. For[6] that newe and highe degrees are alwaies accompanied with greate daingers.[7] Ffor this cause *Virgile* vnder the person of Dido [8] excusethe her tiranie by the newnes of her tytle.

> *Greate neede* (quoth *she*) *and rawe estate of this my*
> *kingdom newe,*
> *Compells me thus my coast to keepe, & wyde about*
> *mee Viewe.*

Neverthelesse let him be soe setled in mynde, that he doe not rashlie beleeue everie rumo*ur* nor moved att everie blast, nor discoorrage himself att [9] everie tryfle, but soe temper his rulle with reason, as neither to greate presumption make him vnwise, or to much distrust intollerable, from hence risethe a question whether it be better for a prince to be beloved [10] or feared, feared or loved, both [11] dowbtlesse are necessarie, but seinge it is harde to make them drawe both in one yoake, I thincke it more safetie, (seinge one must needes be want-inge) to be feared then loved, for this maybe boldlie sayde of men, that they are vngratefull, inconstante, discemblers, fearefull of dayngers, covetous of gayne.[12] When thow shalt deserve well of them, but have noe neede of them, then will they all be thy followers, spende their bludd in thy cause, their good*es*, their lives, their famelyes, but yf extremities happen (as I have often [13] sayde) thow shalt have them to seeke. A prince that trusteth to their promises and taketh their fayre woord*es* for warrantey of their good will*es*, shall not slyp onlie in the foote, but fall downe hedlonge, for frendshipp*es* which are purchased by benefitt*es*, (not ver-tues,) are boughte by good tournes, and yet in tyme of neede will not serve [14] anie turne. Moreover men care lesse to of-fende those that studie to be beloved, then those w*h*ich prac-tise to be feared, for love is conteyned vnder dutie, w*h*ich for verie lighte occasion wicked men will violate, abusinge all

meanes of pietie for anie kynde of proffitte. But dread of punishmente causethe them not onlie to shake for feare, but to
stande faste in obedience; yet lett a prince soe be feared, that
thoughe he cannot wynn their hartes, yet he avoyde their
hatred*es*.[15] For [16] he maie easilie both not be hated, and yet
feared, yf he abstayne from his subiects wealthe, and vse no
violence to the women. But yf the lawes allott anie to deathe,
lett him dare to doe anie Justice, soe longe as the causes of
co*m*menda*c*ion and reason appeare manifest. Onlie lett him
alwayes be heedfull that he thrust not his Sythe into his Cittizens Sheaves; for that men rather forgett the deathes of their
paren*tes* then the losse of their possessions. Itt is easye to
fynde meanes to bereave men of their good*es*, for he that be-
gynnes to live by spoyles, devisethe as manie fetches to deceve, as to [f3o] liue, but to thirst [17] after the bludde of anie
man, is not co*m*mon, nor the cause often fownde.

But when a Prince shalbe in anie [18] armye or multitude
of men, he must not care to be reputed [19] cruell, otherwise he
shall neither have them in order or awe fitt to encounter their
Enemyes, or hable to defende themselves. Amonge all the
woorkes of *Haniball* this was not estemed leaste, that havinge
an infinite companie of all Contries in his Armye, and goinge to subdue straingers there never fell either [20] mutenies
emonge his soldiers, or mislykinge agaynst him, w*hi*ch continewed aswell in conques*tes*, as conflictes. This w*i*thowte
dowbte came to passe, (yf one may soe terme it) by his
barbarous cruelltie, w*hi*ch mingled w*i*th other his vertues
made him bothe noble and terrible; and w*i*thowt his [21] stoute-
nes, all other his vertues had ben but vanities. But writers
w*i*th as little advice as reason, sticke not to marvell att the
effectes, and yet to mislyke the causes, co*m*mendinge his
valour, and condempninge his rig*our*; that all other his vertues had not suffised,[22] the example maybe seene in *Scypio,*

a man of noe lesse vertue then valure, whoe with to muche
lenity [23] caused his Armie to rebell against him in *Spayne*,
which *Fabius Maximus* openlie reprehended in the *Senate*,
callinge him the corrupter of Soldiers, and violater of the
warlike discipline of the *Romans*.

This kynde of pittie in processe of tyme had both obscured
the guyfftes and glorie of *Scipio*, yf he had continewed
soe mercifull when he grewe mightie. But obeyinge [24] the
decrees of the *Senate*, the vice was not onlie darkened in him
but accompted a greate vertue. But to the matter that is of
feare and [25] loue, whether it were [26] better to be feared or
loved, this [27] I conclude, that synce the loue of men hangethe
in their owne wylles, their feare on their princes. There is
noe prince that is wise, but will sticke to that he may commaunde, not to that which others maye denye. Kepinge [28]
the swaye in his hande, not in his subiectes heades, this
alwaies provided that he incurr not hate or [29] offence by his
rigour.

Howe princes owght to keepe their
faythe and promises.   *Cap:* 18.

THERE is noe man soe sotted that knowest not, nor soe
shamelesse that will not confesse howe hollie and honorable a thinge itt is for a prince to keepe his faythe and
promise vnviolated, and to leade his lyffe withowt all reprehension.[1] Yet experience hath taught vs, that those Princes
haue had most renowne for their woorthie factes, that have
had leaste regarde of their woordes or faythes,[2] who [3] cir-
cumventinge the symple sorte that did meane playne soothe,
haue [4] surmounted them in dignitie and made them playne
sottes, for seinge there is twoe kyndes of contention or

striffe,[5] the one by lawe the other by force, the first proper
to men, the later to beastes, men must haue recoorse for redresse to the later, yf they cannot recover their righte by the
first. Therefore [6] itt is verie necessarie for a prince to knowe
as well howe to vse the force and subtilty of beastes, as the
faythe and sincerenes of men, which anciente writers haue
in their woorkes [7] covertlie taught vs by affirminge that
Achilles, and many other woorthy princes were brought vpp
and instructed by *Chiron* the *Centaure*, whoe beinge half
a man and half a beaste, might by his preceptes ingraffe in
the myndes, of those younge Princes the nature of both
kindes. Ffor asmuch therefore as it behoves a prince to
counterfeyte the condicions of brute beastes, they shoulde
aboue all other indeavour bothe to imitate [8] the nature of
the *Lyon* [9] and the *Foxe*. For the Lyons take noe regarde of
the trappes and snares of the hunters, and the foxe is to
weake to defende himself from the Woolffe, therefore to
destroye and avoyde crafte and subtile [10] deceipte, itt is necessarie to be hable to playe the *Foxe;* and to resist [11] force, and
to chase away woolves, the *Lyons* strengthe is as needfull.
But they that will onlie imitate the *Lyon*, is as farr from
safetie, as [12] he is from suspition. Therefore a wise [13] and
prudent prince shoulde sticke noe longer to his promise then
maye stande well with his proffitt, nor thincke himself noe
longer bownde, to keape his othe then the cause remaynes
that moved him to sweare.[14] Surelie yf all men were good
[f31] this precepte were naught,[15] yf they were honest this
were hatefull. But seinge they are wicked and deceiptfull,
it behoves a prince by discemblinge to meete with their
malice, and by cunninge to overthrowe their Crafte. And [16]
nowe a prince can never wante occasions to collour the
breache of his promise.

A thousande examples might be brought in for this purpose to shewe howe manie leagues, howe manie truces, howe many promises of late dayes haue ben broken and made voyde by the vnfaythfullnes of princes. And [17] still he had beste successe [18] in his affayres that had beste skill to playe the foxe,[19] but all the skill is to cover and coollour this crafte well, and by fayninge and dissemblinge to sett a fayre var-nishe on his fowle vice, for men generallie are soe simple, and soe much geeven to their present affairs, that a deceaver that can [20] cunninglie conterfeite his purpose, shall never wante subiect*es* on whom he may practise his skill. Therefore a man shoulde be soe well instructed, that he might be hable to meete them att theyr owne weapons, and knowe bothe how to warde and thrust for his best advantage. I will not passe over the late example of *Pope Alexander* [21] the vj^t whoe bendinge his mynde to mischeeffe, employed all his witt to wilines, and accomptinge it well gotten that he had com-passed by crafte never made bones to deceve any man that beleeved him,[22] of whom he mett a greate manie in his tyme. There [23] was never anie man woulde affirme a thinge with more substantiall reasons, or sweare it with more solempne religion, or per*f*oorme it with soe sleight regarde, yet did he reape co*mm*oditie with [24] his crafte, and fownde sownde proffytt by his subtile practises, for he was his craftes maister, and knewe well the devise howe to traine men into his dayngerr. Itt is not therefore soe necessarie for a prince to be indued with all these vertues before recited, as to beare a face and owtwarde shewe as though he were,[25] not soe proffitable to carrie the substance of them in his mynde, as to counter-feit [26] the substau*n*ce of them in his maners. Ffor this I dare affirme, that theise vertuous quallities shall healpe him in his attemptes, that seemes to haue them, and vseth them not, and hynder him asmuch in his enterprises that hath them and doth observe them in all poyntes. Itt is good to seeme pittifull in punishmente, iuste of thy woorde, and courteouse in thy behavio*ur*,[27] and to be soe,[28] but not to haue thy mynde soe preciselie bente to the observation thereof, but that vppon occasion thowe mayeste be contente to practise the contrarie. Itt is vnpossible for a prince, and speciallie such a one as is newlie raysed to that estate, dulie to observe those thinges w*h*ich causeth men to be esteemed vertuous, for he shalbe constrayned spyte of his harte to transgres the bondes of pyttie, faythe, honestie, courtesie and religion: [29] and therefore it is behooffull for him to carrie a mynde & disposition readie to alter w*i*th all weathers, as the variation of fortune shall minister occasion, as to followe the best, and to be vertuous yf he maye, but yf that will not serve, not to be scripulous to followe the contrarie. A prince shoulde observe w*i*th all [30] dilligence and care *tha*t noe woorde sholde passe his mouthe that did [31] not savour of one of these five quallities before mencioned, and wheresoever he were seene or hearde, he should seeme w*i*th greate reverence to extoll and imbrase *Pittie, Fayth Honestie Courtesie & Religion,* and speciallie the laste, for men generallie are carried away w*i*th the shewe of thing*es*, not w*i*th the substance, everie man can see but fewe can iudge, there is noe man but seeth what thow seemest to bee, but fewe can deserne what thow arte indeede. Which fewe dar not gainesay the opinion of the multitude, w*h*ich haue the maiestie of the prince for theire defence. In the Actions of men, & especiallie in princes causes (w*h*ich are not determinable by lawe nor called in question before iudges) the lookers on for the most parte marke the evente not the causes, the ende not the maner of their proceeding*es*. Lett a prince therefore provide [f32] for the safetie of his person and securitie of his estate and never dowbte but by what meanes soever it be doon (soe it cary a shewe of honestie) it shalbe construed to the best, and be thought woorthy of

greate prayse and commendacion,[32] for the common people
are carried away with the semblance of honestie and good
eventes of Actions, and trulie the wholle worlde it is but a
communaltie, for the wiser sorte that can iudge of thinges
aright are placed in such roomes where the multitude cannot
come vnto. I knowe a kinge of our tyme (whom I will not
name,) that will never talke of other thinge then peace faythe
and honestie, but yf he had followed that in his Actions
which he seemed soe much to favour in speeches, perhappes
his power and reputacion had ben cutt shorter err this tyme.

How a prince owght to beware that he
runn neither into contempte nor hatred
of his Subiectes.   Cap: 19.

FFOR asmuche as in discoursinge of the gyftes and quallities of a prince, I have onlie handled att large those that
seeme to be of greatest importaunce; I meane nowe to runn
over the reste altogether breeflye, that a prince may perceve
(as I have partly touched alreadie,) howe necessarie a thinge
it is for the saftie of his estate to avoyde the hatred and contempte of his people and subiectes, which yf he can doe he
is past all daynger. For to be noted of any other infamie, will
never be preiudiciall to the quietnes of his raigne.

The cheeffe thinges as I sayde that ingender the peoples
hatred, is the losse of their wealth, and the ravishinge of their
woemen, for they accompte themselues verie well dealt with
all soe longe as their goodes be spared, and their credittes not
impayred, and then hath the Prince nothinge to dowbte but
the ambition of a fewe which manie wayes with little labour
he maye easily represse.

The thinges that [1] cause a prince to be dispised and contempned[2] are these, yf he be vnsteedfast of[3] his woorde, dissolute of his behaviour, effeminate in his maners, and fearefull in his Actions, and be accompted neither constante in mynde nor resollute in his determinations, all which a Prince ought to flye as serpentes, and shoowne as rockes and[4] shelffes in the Sea, and indevour in his governmente and administration of Iustice to shewe continewallie a certeine Maiestie[5] mixed with a bolde currage, not withowte gravity & constancye, in soe much that the better sorte maie esteeme his woorde for a lawe, and his sentence in iudgmente irrevocable, and also[6] to rayse and continewe that opinion of him in the hartes of his subiectes, that they[7] maie imagine he can neither be abused by frawde, nor altered by flatterie.

The prince that hath once woonn to himself[8] reputacion and accompte emonge his subiectes, neede not feare neither the conspiracies or coniurations of his subiectes att home nor the assaultes or invasions of his Enemyes abroade; for a prince indeede shoulde soe behaue himself in the wholle coorse of his lyffe, that he maybe feared and had in awe of twoe sortes, the one domesticall, the other foreine, the one subiectes, the other straingers, the owtward enemies wilbe kepte vnder yf they perceaue that he is well provided of Armes and well beloved of his frendes, and frendes he shall not wante to take his parte, yf he obserue good discipline emonge his people, and thinges beinge sure abroade, there is noe dowbte of his saftye att home vnlesse he be disturbed by some rebellion or conspiracie.

And though his foreine Enemies shoulde enterprise anie matter against him, soe longe as his provision for the Warrs were sufficiente and his reputacion emonge his people not impayred, (yf he were not wantinge to himself,) he shoulde be hable to beare of the brunte and rage of their furie, & withstande their malice to their owne gayne and glorie, as *Nabis*

(of whom I have made mention) did, whoe was kinge of
Lacedemon.

But put case that all be quiett abroade, then hath the
prince nothinge to care for, but to foresee that noe rebellion
or secrett conspiracie be attempted against him by his subiect*es*,[9] [f33] whereof he neede not to dowbte, yf he incurr
not the hatred and contempte of the multitude, w*h*ich carefullie (as I sayde before) he must studie to avoyde. For[10]
the surest defence and most approved remedie, that a prince
can finde against these mischeeff*es* is to shunn the hatred and
contempte of the comunaltie,[11] for noe man will venter to
take in hande a conspiracie vnles he make this reconinge
w*i*th himself, that the death of the prince wilbe acceptable to
the people. Hee that is otherwise perswaded will never be soe
mad to vndertake soe daingerous an enterprise. The daingers
that conspiratours wrapp them selues in are almost infinite,
w*h*ich is playnelie seene by their ill successe. For[12] manie
haue had the heartes to attempte a conspiracie, but fewe haue
had the happe to atteyne to[13] their purpose, for he that
takes it in hande can doe noe good alone,[14] neither shall they
finde anie fellowe but such as are malcontent*es*, and having
once discovered the seacrett*es* of their[15] harte to anie that
shall fynde himself agreeved, he shall geeue him good occasion
to creepe into creaditt, and to mende[16] his estate. For[17] by
revealinge his purpose he maie redresse his owne povertie,
and seinge the gaine certeyne on the one syde, & the enterprise
daingerous on the other, he must either[18] be a mervalous
frende to the conspirato*u*r or mortall enemye to the prince,
that will conceale the confedracie; to conclude this matter
in fewe woordes, the conspirato*u*rs on their sydes[19] haue
nothinge but feare,[20] mistrust, hard[21] thought*es*, and dreade
of punishment to amaze them. But Princes on their sydes
haue the maiesty of their highe estates, their lawes, the gardes,

and the succour of their frendes to defende them: and yf therew*i*thall they haue the heart*es* and goodwill of the Comunaltie, it is vnpossible that anie man shoulde be fownde soe rashe and madd to [22] conspire against them, for as itt is an ordinarie matter to feare before the fact he co*m*mitted, soe in this case they shall fynde more cause to dreade when their purpose is executed, for havinge by this wicked deede incenced the peoples rage against them, they cannot imagine whither safelie to flye for succo*ur*.

To prove this, a man might bringe a thousande examples, but this one shall suffice that fell owte in our fathers dayes, *Haniball Bentiuoglio*, grandfather to this *Haniball* that nowe is,[23] whoe was Lorde and Prince of *Bononia*, beinge murthered by the *Canescanes*, w*h*ich conspired against him, leavinge noe children behynde him but *John* his Soonne an infante in his cradle. The Comunaltie rose streyght at the [24] reporte of this haynous murder, and putt all the ffamilie of *Canescanes* to the sworde, w*h*ich grewe vppon non [25] other cause then vppon the goodwill and co*m*mon [26] affection w*h*ich the people did beare to the house and race of the *Bentiuoglians*, w*h*ich was soe greate, that when there was non lefte of that familie to governe them, receivinge intelligence that there was att *Florence* a younge man discendid [27] of the ancient lyne and stocke of the *Bentiuoglians*, whoe vntill that tyme was thought to be a Smythes Soonne, they sente for him and putt the governmente of their Cittie, and them selues into his handes, whoe ruled over them vntill such tyme, as their younge Prince came vnto lawfull age to sway the sworde himself. To shutt vpp this matter a prince (soe longe as he hath the heart*es* of the co*m*mon people [28]) neede not to dowbte the daynger of conspiracies,[29] but yf they be offended he hath iust cause to feare. Yf they hate his person, he [30] may catch harme by their practises. In states well governed, wise princes haue alwayes had a speciall care to doe nothinge that might cause the nobilitie to dispayre of their safetie, nor leaue anie thinge vndoon that might gayne the goodwill*es* of the co*m*munaltie, and keepe them in quiete and due obedience, and this is even the matter of greatest importaunce that a prince hath to thincke on or to occupie his heade w*i*thall.

Amonge those kingdomes w*h*ich in *our* dayes are thought to be well ordered and wislie governed the Realme of *Fraunce* is reckoned for one, where there are manie good and pollitique orders established, as well for the libertie of their kinges pleasure, as the assuraunce of his person, the cheeffe whereof is their perliamente and the authoritie thereof, w*h*ich was invented by the first fownders of that kingdom, whoe knowing the ambition and pride of the nobillitie, thought good to provide a bridle to restrayne their insolencie; and considering the naturall hatred that is ingraffed in the heart*es* of the Co*m*mons against the nobillitie, p*r*oceedinge of a feare w*h*ich they [f34] haue of them, (beinge desirous to provide for their securitie) would not leaue the burthen thereof vppon the kinge, that he might not therby purchase the displeasure of the Nobillitie by takinge parte w*i*th the weake, nor incurr the hatred of the co*m*munaltye by leauinge to much to the greate men. Therefore [31] they ordeyned this p*a*rliamente as a thirde Iudge betwene bothe, that might [32] (w*i*thowt callinge the king*es* affection to their partie [33] in question) represse the insolencie of the one, and redresse the iniuryes of the other. There [34] coulde nothinge be invented w*i*th greater iudgment to the co*m*mon quiett of the Realme, or greater care for the safetie of the prince then this. Here hence wee maie gather a principle [35] well woorthy the notinge, that princes shoulde dispatch those thing*es* by their deputyes w*h*ich will move envie, and execute those thing*es* themselues which will merritt thanckes. To conclude againe, a Prince ought to maintaine and vpholde the reputacion of the nobillitie, but yet soe that [36] the Communaltie goe not to wracke, nor haue iust cause to hate him. Manie perhappes doe imagyne that they can bringe examples to disprove my opinion. Ffor lookinge to the lives of manie Emperours of *Roome*, they fynde som that haue lived noblye and haue ben men of singuler coorrage and valure, and yet notwithstandinge, haue loste their Empires by force of their Enemyes or their lives by the malice of Conspiratours; but beinge desirous therefore [37] to aunsweare vnto such obiections as maybe broughte against me, [38] I meane to examine the manners and disposition of some of those Emperours, and searche owt the cause why they had such ill successe, which I will prove shall not be vnlyke those reasons which I haue already alleaged, and by the waye I will propose such noble actes of those daies to be considered of, as shalbe woorthy the notinge of suche as shall reade them. Itt shall suffice me to entreate onlie of those Emperours which succeed [39] in the Empire from *Marcus Aurelius* the Philosopher to *Maximinus*, which are these, the first *Marcus* and his Soonne *Commodus*, *Pertinax*, [40] *Iulianus*, *Seuerus*, *Antonius* and *Caracalla* his soonne, *Alexander* & *Maximinus*. These are first to be observed, that whereas in other kingdomes and Commonwealthes there is but one kynde of Variaunce & striffe to be deserned, that is the ambition of the nobilitie, and the harebraynd hastines of the Communalltie; the [41] Romaine Emperours were trowbled with a thirde mischeef, for they were to indure the crueltie and covetousnes of the Soldiers which (beinge a matter of greate difficultie) was the cause of manie of their distructions, for it was a cause that required noe small Iudgment to contente the myndes both of the soldiers, and of the people, the one sorte desiringe to leade their lives in peace and quietnes and therf*ore* loved a prince that was of a gentle and curteouse disposition: and contrarywise [42] the other imbrased a prince that was of a warlyke nature geeven to insolencie cruelty and spoylinge, all w*h*ich they provoked him to execute vppon the people, thereby to dooble their owne paye and satisfie their covetousnes and barbarous in-humanitie, hereof it came to passe that those Empero*u*rs that coulde neither by nature nor arte, gayne that reputac*i*on emongst them, that they were hable to bridle the owtrage of both sortes, and keepe their neck*es* vnder yoake, were sure by one faction to be vtterlie overthrowen; But the greatest nombers of these Empero*u*rs especiallie of them that were newlie raysed not by succession but election to that dignity, wayinge w*i*th themselues the contrarie nature of these kyndes of people and diversitie of their humo*u*rs, [43] inclynded their mynd*es* to please the Soldiers, not respectinge the iniuries that were doon to the people wh*i*ch was the beste councell they could take. Ffor when princes cannot choose but that they must incurre the displeasure of soome, they shoulde first indeavo*u*r to keepe in w*i*th the multitude, and yf they cannot compasse that, lett them be sure to take parte w*i*th the strongest syde, and keepe them their ffrend*es*. This caused manie Empero*u*rs, (wh*i*ch for the slender tytle and rawe estate w*h*ich they had in the Empire needed extraordi-narie favo*u*r and frendshipp) to inclyne more willinglie to the Soldiers then to the People, wh*i*ch turned to their gayne or losse accordinge as the Princes themselues had skill to vse their authoritie and maintaine their reputacion emongst [44] them, hereof it came to passe, that *Marcus Pertinax* & *Alex-ander* that were men very mylde and modest in their be-havio*u*rs, [45] Lovers of Iustice, enemyes to crueltie, endued with all clemencie and courtesie, had all sorrowfull and vnfortunate endes. But onlie *Marcus* whoe lived farr more noblie then the rest, and dyed more honorablie, for he came by the [f35] Empire by lawfull succession, and therefore had noe cause to currie favo*ur* either with the Soldiers or co*m*munalty, atteyninge his authoritie withowte their ayde, and his soverayntie withowt their service. Besyde that he was accompanied with soe many vertues w*h*ich made him to be both [46] reverenced and feared, that in all his lyffe he gave neither parte cause [47] to hate or˙ contempne him, and yet keapte them all within compasse of theyr dutie and obedience. But *Pertinax* was chosen Empero*ur* againste the goodwill [48] of the soldiers, whoe beinge accustomed to live licenciouslie vnder the goverment of Co*m*modus, coulde not away with that honest and temperate kynde of lyffe wherevnto he sought to bringe them. Soe by this meanes purchasinge their hatred, and by reason of his age fallinge into contempte, he loste both his lyffe and empyre att the verie beginninge of his governmente; whereof [49] may be gathered that ill will maybe gotten aswell by vertue as by vice. Wherefore a Prince that will mainteine himself safe in his state, shalbe constrayned somtymes to degresse from vertue and the perfect rulles of Iustice. Ffor yf those [50] (whether they be the co*m*mon people, or the soldiers, or the noblemen) whose ayde and assistau*n*ce he cannot wante withowte preiudice of his estate, and apparante daynger of his saftie, be viciously geeven and wickedlie bente, he shalbe enforced to followe their humo*ur*s, and allowe of their lewdnes. For [51] honestie in such a case woulde hurte him, and verteous dealinge woulde be his vtter decaye.

But lett vs come to *Alexander*, whoe was indued with manie good partes, in whose mynde vprighte deallinge seemed to haue made her seate, in soe much that amonge other co*m*mendacions [52] that are ascribed vnto him, it is reported that in xiij yeares (which was the tyme that he ruled the Romane

Empire) noe man was putt to deathe but by sentence of lawe. Nothwithstandinge because he was thoughte to be of an effeminate mynde, and to much lead by his mothers Councell, he fell in contempte of his soldiers, and was slayne by their conspiracie. And nowe on the other syde lett vs consider the manner [53] and behaviour of *Comodus Seuerus Antonius, Caracalla* and *Maximinus*, and wee shall fynde them as cruell as he was courteous, murderinge where he shewed mercie, and spoylinge all in their greedie rage that had ben spared in his gentle raigne, whoe to satisfie the insatiable covetousnes of their soldiers, abstayned from noe iniurie that mighte be inflicted on the People and yet everie one of them exceptinge *Seuerus* came to vntimlie deathes and vnfortunate endes. Ffor *Seuerus* was of that boulde currage, and noted to be of that singuler valure & prowesse, that havinge woon the heartes of his soldiers, although it was doon with great hurte of his Subiectes, he was able to keepe and maintaine himself and his Empire in floorishinge [54] estate withowt dainger. For his magnanimitie and other excellent vertues appered soe playnlie both in the sight of his soldiers, and the other common people, that the one sorte beinge astonied att his Maiestie and the other reverensinge his authoritie, were both kept in dewtifull obedience. And for asmuch as princes deedes are woorthy greate admiracion. I will declare howe well for his advantage he coulde conterfeite both the *fox* and the *lyon*, whose natures and properties (as I saide [55]) are to be imitated by greate princes.

Seuerus knowinge howe little accompte there was made att *Rome* of *Iulianus* the Emperour by reason of his sluggishe and dull nature, perswaded the Armie over which he was generall in *Iliria*, [56] that they coulde not doe better then goe [57] to *Roome* to revenge the death of Pertinax, whoe was slayne by the Imperiall garde, vnder this Colour (not manifestinge

the pretence he had to aspire to the Empire.[58]) he caused his
Armie to marche towarde [59] Rome, and was in *Italy* before it
was knowen, he was come owte of *Iliria*: When he came to
Rome, the Senate for feare putt *Iulianus* to deathe, and chose
him Emper*our* in his steede, after this good beginninge there
was twoe blockes to be removed owte of his waye ere he
could enioye the wholle Empire as he wolde, the one in
Asia,[60] where one *Niger* cheeffe Generall in the easte partes
caused himself to be saluted by the name of Emper*our*, the
other in the west, where *Albinus* pretended the lyke tytle,
and indeavored alsoe to compasse it. But consideringe howe
daingerous it was to professe himself an open enemy to them
bothe at once, he ditermined to suppresse *Niger* [61] by force
lyke a lyon, and to circumvent *Albinus* by subtiltie like a
foxe. He wroate therefore vnto him, that whereas the rule
and government of the Empire was conferred vppon him
by the conscente of the Senate, he purposed to make him
partner of his good fortune, and sending [62] [f36] the tytle of
Cæsar by the dewe of the *Senate*, chose him to be his asso-
ciate and companion in the Empire, all w*h*ich was taken
verie thanckfullye and in great good parte by *Albinus*, as
yf they had ben soe indeede. But *Seuerus* havinge overcom
Niger, and taken good order in the Easterne [63] Contries for
his affaires, cominge backe to Rome, made a greevous com-
playnte to the *Senate* against *Albinus*, whom he pretended
to haue conspired his deathe by treason; nothwithstandinge
all the favo*u*rs and frendship*es* [64] that he had receaved by
his meanes, and therefore besought that w*i*th their conscent*es*
and assistaunce he might goe thither to take dewe punishment of this [65] ingratitude, soe goinge into *Fraunce* he berefte
him at one tyme both of his lyffe, and Empire.

Hee therefore that w*i*th iudgment will consider of this
mans doinge shall fynde him both a cruell Lyon and a craftie

Fox, and that he was feared and reverenced of all that either [66] knewe him, or heard of his name; he [67] vsed soe good discipline in his Campe, that his Soldiers never hated him for his crueltie, nor contempned him for anie imperfection; which [68] made him hable to welde the charge of soe greate an empire thoughe he came newlie by it, for his greate maiestie & reputacion ridd him from the dowbte of the Commmon peoples hatred, which by oppression he had iustlie deserved.

His Soonne *Antonius* was likwise accompted of greate valure and wisdom and had such speciall gyftes as made him honored of all the worlde for his maiestie, and loved of his Soldiers for his affability, for he was a right warriour patiente to indure [69] any labour contempninge all dayntie fare, and dellicate fynenes which woon the soldiers hartes, and caused them to followe him. Notwithstandinge in the Ende he grewe to that savage inordinate and vnknowen [70] Crueltie, (for beside manie other greate and principall matters, he putt to the swoorde the greatest parte of the people of *Rome* and all the wholle Cittie of *Alexandria*) that he was hated generally of all [71] men, in soe much that his neerest frendes, and those that were his garde begann to feare him. Att last a Centurian slewe him in the middest of his owne Armie, whereby wee may note that a prince cannot prevent the mischeef, or escape the dainger, when one that is obstinate in his purpose & resollute in his ditermination, [72] hath conspired his deathe, for he that is carelesse of his owne lyffe, maye easilie putt an other man to deathe. But a prince hath little cause to dowbte this kynde of deathe, for that [73] it is seldom seene, that anie wilbe soe desperate. Onlie this he is to foresee that he doe not greevouslie offende or extreame iniure [74] anie such man, whose service he must after vse abowte his owne person or councell, in the administracion of his kingdom or Empire, into which errour *Antonius* ran head-

longe, for he had putt to deathe the brother of the saide
Centurian a little before most shamfullie and with greate dis-
pight, and everie daye threatened that he shoulde drincke
of the same Cupp, and notwithstandinge reteyned him as one
of his cheeffe guarde; wherein he shewed himself rashe without either good advise or councell, which (as it fell owte
afterwarde [75]) cost him his lyffe. But nowe lett vs speake a
little of *Commodus*, whoe might haue keapte his Empire
with little care, which he did gett with soe little coste. Ffor
beinge the soonne of *Marcus Aureli*us he succeeded [76] in the
Empire as heire to his ffather: and yf [77] he had inherited his
condicions as he did his Crowne, or followed his footstepes
as he did his owne follie, he had satisfied the expectacion of
the people and pleased the humours of the Soldiers, but he beinge of a blockyshe witte and yett of a cruell disposition, gaue
himself wholly to please the soldiers, the raynes of whose
licencious myndes he lett loose, the better to please their
heartes and exersise his owne tiranye in oppressinge the
people, but havinge noe reguarde to defend his honour, nor
vpholde his reputacion, but shewinge himself oftentymes [78]
vppon the stages to fighte with fencers, and committinge
other base partes, vnfitt for the maiestie of the empire, hee
became contemptible and a vearie abiecte in the sighte of his
Soldiers; and soe beinge hated in the contrie of his Subiectes,
and contempned in the Campe of his soldiers, they conspired
against him, and put him to deathe. Itt remaynes [79] nowe that
wee speake so somwhat of the nature & disposition of *Maxi-*
minus, he lykewise was a verie martiall man. And when the
people began to loathe his effeminate lyffe, and the soldiers
to mislyke the idle mynde of *Alexander*, of whom I haue
made mencion before, they conspired his deathe and chose
this man Emperour in his place, which he did not longe
enioye, for twoe thinges brought him into hatred and Con-

tempte; the one because he was a man of a verie base condicion, for he had been once a shepheard in *Thrasia*, which
beinge notoriouslie knowen, made him notablie contempned.
The other was, for that att his first enteraunce into his royall
government, he deferred his goinge to *Rome*, & [f37] purchased the suspicion of a tyrante,[80] er he was setled in his
throne, for he sufferred his generalles and deputies aswell att
Roome, as in all other places and provinces, grevouslie to
oppresse the people with spoyles and extortions. Soe he
became odious to all men, and then some contemninge him
for the basenes of his birthe and educacion, and other hat-
inge him for the crueltie of his nature and disposition, first
Africa, then the *Senate* and people of *Rome*, and lastlie all
Italie rose against him. Vppon this his Armye that was then
encamped before *Aquila*, seinge the Citty impregnable, and
his crueltie vnsupportable, and perceavinge howe manie
Enemyes he had bothe att home, and abroade, conspired
against him, and putt him to deathe.

I will speake nothinge of *Heliogabalus, Macrinus*, nor
Iulianus, whoe beinge contemned, dispised and abiectlie
thoughte of, were all putt to the swoorde ere they were
warme in their seates, but I will drawe to a conclusion in
these matters, and this is my opinion, that Princes of our
tyme in rulinge their kingdoms, and principalities, are not
forced to vse anie[81] such extraordinarie favour to their
Soldiers: for though there be some regarde to be had of
them, yet princes are not tyed to those extremities that those
Emperours were. For[82] there be noe bandes of soldiers or
armies nowe adayes, that keepe soe continewallie together,
and waxe olde in the govermente of Provinces, as those of
the *Romaine Empire* were accustomed to doe. Therefore yf
in those dayes there was more respect to be had of the
soldiers then the other Subiectes because they were the

Stronger, nowe contrariewise Princes [83] shoulde rather seeke
to please the people because they are the mightier, I except
the greate Turke [84] and the Soldan of *Egipte*, and *Siria.* The
greate *Turke* enterteyneth abowte him xij thousande footemen and xvi thousande horsmen, in whom the strength and
securitie of him self, & his empyre [85] doth consist, and therefore it is greate reason, he should favour them more then the
common people. The *Souldans* [86] estate is much lyke this,
whoe placinge his safetie in lyke manner in his soldiers
handes, cares not greatlie for the Communaltie, soe as he may
wynn [87] their heartes; yet the *Souldans Empyre* differreth
from the *Turkes,* and variethe from the maner of other
princes estates, drawinge more nere to the nature of the
popedome, neither discendinge by inheritaunce, nor may be
properlie termed newe. Children of the princes succeede not
the fathers, but such as are chosen by the authoritie, and
consent of the electours, which manner waxinge olde by
tyme, cannot be called newe, besydes it is not incombred
with those difficultyes, that newe principalityes are subiecte
vnto. Ffor thoughe the prince himself be newe, yet the lawes
and orders wherevnto he is tyed are anciente, which admitt
him for their prince, and imbrase his goverment as yf he
had come by it by inheritance.

But to come to our purpose, he that with iudgment will
consider of the examples which wee haue broughte, and
obserue such notes as wee haue gathered by these accidentes,
shall easilie perceaue that all their mischeeffe, and mishappes
that ever befell anie of those Emperours had noe other roote,
but hatred and contempte,[88] & be [89] alsoe able to iudge from
whence it proceeded; that some of these Emperours followinge one kynde of govermente and some an other, yet of
both sortes there were some that had good successe, and
some badd, for it was hurtfull for *Pertinax* and *Alexander*

which were raysed newlie to their dignities by election to imitate the clemencie of *Marcus;* and it turned *Caracalla* and *Commodus* [90] to as greate damage [91] to practise the crueltie of Severus. Ffor none of them were indued with that vertue and currage, that they were hable to followe their foote-steppes arighte. Wherefore a prince that is newlie raysed to his estate, in keapinge thereof can neither imitate altogether [92] the deedes of *Marcus Aurelius,* nor make *Seuerus* his Paterne to followe in all poyntes, but must learne of *Seuerus* such pollecyes, as maye serve for to [93] confirme and establishe his estate. And [94] of *Marcus* such vertues, as he must vse in de-fendinge and governinge the same.

Whether fortresses & other thinges which princes practise for the safty of their estates be profitable, or hurtfull.   *Cap:* 20.

SOME Princes the better to keepe their dominions in safetie, and their Contries in subiection haue disfurnishte the people of their weapons, and spoyled them of their Armour. Others [1] haue continewed factions att home, and manie haue nourished Enemyes abroade, some haue buylded Castles & fortresses, and others haue raysed and pulled them quyte downe. For [2] fewe haue bente their myndes to com-passe their frendshipp, whose faythes they suspected att their entrance into their raigne. And although noe man be hable to putt downe an absolute opinion of them all, vnlesse he descende to perticulers, and that the question were moved of soome one speciall place, yet will I handle them all in a generall discourse, soe well as [f38] my skyll and the mat-ter it self will suffer mee.

It was never seene that a prince newlie raysed to his

estate did ever disfurnishe his subiectes of their armour and
weapons, but rather yf he did get dominion over those that
were unarmed and naked people, he straight indeavored to
trayne them vpp in military disciplyne, for he may boldlie
trust those whom he traynes vpp himself, whose examples
will cause them to be faythfull that before were [3] suspected,
and confirme their loves that before were loyall, and finallie
to cause all his subiectes to take his parte: and for asmuch as
noe prince is able to arme all his people, yf he deserve well
of those that are trayned, he may vse the rest att his pleasure,
whose cunninges were never tryed, and makinge this difference betwene them, he shall haue those bownde to him that
taste his liberalitie, and not offende the rest to whom he is
not soe bountifull. Ffor they themselues will excuse him; and
thincke it greate reason, that those that take the greatest
payne, shoulde lykwise tast of greatest proffitt. But yf he
spoyle his people of their armour and wepons, he offerreth
them greate iniurie, for either he must thincke them such
Cowardes that he will not trye them, or such cutthroates
that he dare not trust them, and soe either contemninge their
force, or condemninge their faythe, he shalbe sure to purchase their hatred. And seinge noe prince can protect his
estate withowt the force of Armes, he shalbe driven to hyre
strayngers, that mistrustes his owne. And [4] of what momente
and force they are, is alreadie declared at large, and thoughe
some of them be good, yet are they not of sufficiente power
to defende him from the invasion of a mightie Enemie, or
the insurrection of his owne people, when the one for hate
and the other for hope shall attempte anie matter against
him. Therefore a prince newlie raysed to his estate, must be
sure to haue in his newe principalitie a sufficient armie (well
trayned) of his owne people and subiectes, for prooffe
whereof almoste everie historie is full of Examples.

But yf a prince shall happen to wyn anie newe province which he doth annexe to his Empire, as parte of his aunciente inheritance, then shoulde he take bothe armes and weapons from all the inhabitantes, exceptinge onlie such as assisted him in the conquest thereof, and those in processe of tyme he shoulde weaken by little & little as occasions served, vntill he had lefte them in a maner naked, and this shoulde be his care that in everie province of his dominion he should haue soldiers of his owne naturall subiect*es*, such as were borne and bredd in that parte of his dominions, that hath ben longe vnder the govermente of him and his ancestors.[5]

Itt hath ben a common example emongst *our* Ancestors at *Florence* and such as haue [6] ben accompted vearie wise men that the cytie of *Pistoria* was to be kepte by factions, and the Cittye of *Pysa* by Fortress*es*. Hereof it came to passe that in manie cyttyes vnder their dominion they maynteyned stryffe [7] and dissentions that they might the easier keepe them in subiection.

This might be well doon in those dayes, when *Italy* was full of trowbles and tossed vpp and downe, backward and forward with everie wave of vnconstante fortune. But att this daye I thincke that [8] councell would prove vnproffitable altogether.[9] Ffor I cannot be perswaded that quarrell*es* can breede anie commoditie, but I rather thincke that such contentions in a Cittye doe open wyde gapp*es* for the entrance of the Enemye, for the weker sorte [10] will alwayes ioyne with them, and then the stronger shall not be able to withstande their force beinge to weake to susteyne the charge and assaulte, both of their foreine foes and domestical Enemyes.

The *Venetians* induced as I thincke by the former occasions [11] mayntayned the factions of the *Guelfi*,[12] & *Gibellini* in certeine Cittyes of their Empyre, and although they never sufferred it to growe to slaughter or open hostilitie, yet they still added oyle to the burninge lampes [18] of their hatred, that the peoples heades beinge occupyed abowte questions of their controversyes, might haue noe leasure to attempte anie thinge, against the quiett of their Common wealthe, which succeeded not (as it well appered) accordinge to their expectation; for when they were overthrown att *Vayla*,[14] the one parte took harte att grasse,[15] shooke of their yoke contemninge their authoritie and denyinge them obedience.

Theis devises of goverment doe bewraye the weaknes of the prince that vseth them. Therefore he that is of sufficient power to rule his dominion, will never allowe such dissentions in his Cittyes. In tyme of peace they maye stande in some steede, whille by their brawles others maybe better ruled, but yf warres arise the slendernes of *tha*t shifte wilbe quicklie seene. [f39]

Withoute dowbte princes become greate and famous by atchivinge dayngerouse enterprises and by removinge such hinderances by force as stood betwene them and their fame. And therefore fortune when shee is disposed to rayse the glory of any man especially of a prince that is newly clymbed to his Crowne (whoe hath more neede of reputation then he that comes by his kyngdome by inheritaunce) will stirr vpp enemyes against him, and provide exploytes fytt to increase his honour that he overcominge such adventures as occasions [16] offerrs him to vndertake, he may clymbe higher by the same ladder [17] which his Enemyes haue brought him, wherefore many haue thought it a poynte of greate pollicy in [18] a prince when he fyndes occasion to pyke quarrelles of purpose with som weake Enemyes that by overcoming them, his power maybe talked of, and his name thought more terrible.

Som princes newly raysed to their estates haue fownde more faythe in the promise,[19] and more proffitt in the service of such as they suspected att their enteraunce into their raigne, then in those in whom they reposed greatest truste. *Pandulphus Petrusi*us *Prince of Siena* governed his dominion rather by those whom he suspected then anie other.

I cannot speake much of this kynde of Govermente, because it varyes accordinge to the nature of the place where, and the persons emonge whom it is vsed. Only this I will say yf[20] those men w*h*ich at the beginninge of a Princes reigne were his suspected enemyes, be such as wante force to supporte their[21] owne faction, it shalbe an easy matter for him to reconsyle them and make them his frendes, and they must need*es* shewe themselues more forwarde in his service to ridd them owte of *th*at suspic*i*on that was conceved against them, and so it comes to passe that the prince is better served by such then by those whoe standinge vppon termes of their former fidelity, seeke not to incruse their credit by their duty or dilligence. And seing I am entred into this matter I thincke it necessarie to admonishe a Prince that hath newly gotten a Province by the ayde and assistance of the Inhabitantes, to[22] consider deepely and advisedly w*i*th himself, what cause moved them to take his parte and to further his enterprise, and yf he fynde that they[23] did it not for some speciall hope they had of hym, but for the spightfull hate they did beare theyr other Prynce, he shall alsoe feele[24] it a matter of greate difficulty, and full of troble to continewe their frendshipp, for he shall never be able to satisfy their expectac*i*on. The cause of this beinge sought owt and examined by such examples as maybe gathered owt of anciente writers, & newe;[25] It will appere a far more easie matter for a prince to wyn the favo*u*r of those that withstoodd his enterprise and were Enemyes to his Conquest, then welde their frendshipp that furthered his purpose, and overthrowe the state of their Province, for the spight they did beare to their Prince. It hath ben an ancient custom emonge princes, the better to keepe their contryes and dominions in quietnes to buylde castles, towers & ffortress*es,* w*h*ich as chaynes and bridles, might tye and [26] restraine, such as woulde attempt any thinge against them: and that they might haue place of refuge to w*i*thdrawe themselues saflye into yf any sodaine violence and mischeef vnlooked for were offerred them. I will not condemne this councell nor disalowe the devise,[27] because it is verie anciente and vsuall. Yet [27a] notw*i*thstandinge wee haue seen in o*u*r tyme *Nicholas Vitellius* Rase and overthrowe twoe fortresses in the Cittie of *Castello,* the better to keepe the people thereof in subiection,[28] and *Guydus Vbaldus* [29] Duke of *Vrbine* having recovered his Estate from whence *Valentinus* [30] had shooved him [31] by force, overthrewe and defaced all the bulwoorkes and fortress*es* w*i*thin his province, thinckinge by that meanes he shoulde be hable the better to continewe his possession.

The *Bentiuoglij* did the lyke, when they recovered the Citty of *Bononia.* Fortresses therefore are proffitable accordinge to the diversitie of tymes. Yf [32] they pleasure thee one waye, they offende thee an other.

To conclude this maybe sayde of them, they maye stande a prince in good steede that lives more in dowbte of his owne people then of straingers; but he that feareth straingers more then his owne Subiectes hath noe neede of them. The *Castle of Millayne* buylte by *Francis Sforza* was more preiudiciall to his successo*u*rs, and turned them to greater losse and trowble, than any other Erro*u*r that ever he co*m*mitted in the tyme of his goverment, therefore the surest bulwoorke or fortresse that a Prince can haue, is to shvnn and avoyde the hatred of the multitude. [f40] Ffor yf he haue once incenced

their furye there are noe fortresses soe stronge that can defende him from their force, for yf his owne subiect*es* be
once [33] vpp in Armes he shalbe sure of Forreine Enemyes
redy to take their partes, it was never observed in *our* tyme
that fortresses or stronge holdes [34] turned anie prince to good,
but only the Countesse of [35] Furley after the deathe of the
Earle *Hieronimus* her housbande, for therby shee escaped
the furye of the people, stayed for the ayde of the *Millaynes,*
and in the ende recovered her estate agayne, for the tyme
fell owte soe then, that noe other Prince coulde com to assist
the People: but such strengthe coulde [36] not defende her,
when *Valentinus* invaded her dominion, and her owne
people ioyned with him to revenge the olde iniuryes. Therefore it had ben much better for her to haue avoyded the
hatred of her subiect*es* then to haue trusted to the strengthe
of her Fortresses.

These thinges considered I allowe aswell of those that
buylde Fortresses, as of those that care not for them, onlye
I mislyke of suche, as puttinge confidence in their castles, doe
lightlie esteme the hatred of their people.

*Howe a prince oughte to behaue himselfe to winne
    reputacion.*   *Cap:* 21.

THERE is nothinge that more co*m*mendethe the person of
a prince then to excell aboue all other men aswell in
enterprises of worthye attemptes, as in examples of rare and
singuler vertue.[1] In this *our* tyme wee haue *Ferdinando* of
Aragon nowe kinge of *Spayne* whom a man maye call a
newe Prince, seinge from the weake power of a kinge he hath
soe incresed in glorie and renowme, that he is becom the
most puissant of all christian Princes. He that will but take

viewe of his actes, shall fynde them all excellente and som paste the creditt of common experience.

In the beginninge of his raigne he invaded the kingdom of *Granada* [2] which enterprise was the roote of his renowme and grownde of all his glorye, for thereby he delivered his owne contrye from daynger and removed such blockes as might hinder his purpose, and keepe besydes the myndes of his *Barrons* of Castilia occupyed, which whilst they thoughte vppon those warrs had noe leasure to rayse anie newe trowbles, or thincke vppon anie frawde though [3] they sawe their neighbours house on fyre,[4] but in the meane tyme when Hee fownde oportunitie he turned his power vppon them, woonn their Contry vppon the sodaine and brought them all into subiection. He handled the matter soe that the churche of *Roome* and the people of his owne contrie defrayed the charge of his armye, [5] by meanes of longe warres his soldiers became soe experte that he obteyned manie glorious victoryes, which made him both mightie and famous.

Moreover that he might better attempte greate matters vnder coollour of his affection which he did beare to christian Religion, he determined to practise a holie kynde of crueltie, in banishing and expellinge owte of his contrie the wholle generation of the Iewes: which was a strainge and woonderfull example, vnder coollour of this godly pretence, he invaded Affrica, made a voyage into *Italie,* and lastlie assaulted Ffraunce, and soe notablie enterprised newe and notable attemptes, and helde the myndes and thoughtes of his Subiectes woonderinge att the effectes of that which he had [6] doonn, and expectinge the eventes [7] of that which [8] he tooke in hande. Those his [9] deedes did soe springe one owte of an other, that the people never had leasure to attempte anie thinge against hym.

It is alsoe expedient for a prince in his Government, to doe some suche thinge in the administration of Iustice as may move admiracion in the mynd*es* of his subiect*es*, as *Bernardus* of *Millayne* was woonte to doe, namely when occasion hath brought into his hand*es* some man that for his good or bad desert*es* meriteth an extraordinarie requitall then to devise that his punishment maybe soe extreame, or his preferment soe excellente that it may administer [10] sufficient matter for the people to talke of a greate whille after. Aboue althing*es* lett a prince indeavo*ur* in all the Actions and coorse of his lyffe to shewe himself worthy of the tytle of soe greate hono*ur*.

Itt is alsoe verie co*m*mendable in a prince to shewe himself either a professed frende, or an open enemy, that is to saye to be resollute to take parte w*i*th one syde, w*hi*ch is a much saffer waye, then to shewe him self a newter. Ffor yf twoe mighty men that are borderers vppon his kingdom fall att variaunce and goe together by the eares, eyther he hath cause to feare him that shalbe Conquero*ur* or he neede not care, in both cases it is his saffest waye, [f41] to enter into Armes and to professe himself a frende to one partie: [11] in the firste yf he doe not he shalbe a praye for the conquero*ur* and never pytied of him that is overcom. Neither [12] hathe he anie righte or reason to alleage for himself why he shoulde either be defended [13] or releeved of either parte; for the Conquero*ur* will contemne such suspected frend*es* as refused to ayde him in tyme of neede. and he that is overcom hath noe reason to succour him that did leave him succourlesse in his greatest extremity.

Antiocus came into *Greece* by the procuremente of the *Etolians* to thrust owte the *Romans*. Att his cominge he sente his Ambassado*ur*s to the *Achaians* that were confedrat*es* w*i*th the *Romanes*, requesting them to take neither parte, the *Romans* on the other syde perswaded them to take vpp armes and to come to their succours. When the *Senate* of the *Achaians* were sett to deliberate of this matter, the Ambassadour of the *Romanes* exceptinge against him, replyed on this sorte. That which he affirmes to be best for yow and most proffitable for your commonwealthe (to wytt) that yow shoulde not meddle with our warres is the onlie thinge that will bring your faythe in suspition with vs, and your contrie in subiection to them. Ffor yf withowt pleasuringe or reguarde to anie partie yow absteine from the warr, yow shalbe lefte destitute as a rewarde to the conquerour. This is an infallible rule, that he that is leaste thy frende will always [14] request to inclyne to neither syde, and he that loves thee best will perswade thee to take vpp thy weapons and shewe thy self in the Fyelde; but Princes that are not resollute sekinge onlie to shvnn the present perill, behave themselues lyke newters which manie tymes is the cause of their vtter over throwe.

But when a prince corragiously taketh parte with one syde,[15] yf his frende overcom them (though he be made soe mightie that he shalbe [16] driven to stande at his mercy) yet notwithstandinge he hath entred a good bande of Frendshipp with hym, loue is ioyned betwene them, and men are not soe farr past grace and goodnes, that by the example of soe greate ingratitude, they will practise his ruyne, that was the cause of their rysinge, and besyde that victories are not soe happely gotten, but that the conquerour shalbe constrayned to haue some respect, speciallie of Iustice & equitie.

But nowe [17] yf thy ffrende take the foyle and the Enemy gett [18] the goale, yet hast thow gotten a frende that will sticke to thee to the vttermost of his power, and take thy parte in all fortunes, and soe perhapes in the ende yow may werie owte the Conquerour and recover your losse.[19]

In the seconde case when those that are vpp in armes be such, that a prince neede not care whether parte gett the victorie, yet then is it greate wisdom to ioyne with one syde, for by the ayde of the one thow shalt be bane of the other, and soe when the victory is gotten it shall remayne att thy disposition, and the victorie must needes fall on his syde whom thow doste ayde in the quarrell.

Here a prince must take greate heede that vnlesse vrgent necessitie enforce him, he succour not one that is stronger then himself to oppresse anie other, for when the other is overcome, thowe thy self shall stande to the conquerours mercy which is an inconvenience which all [20] princes shoulde carefully avoyde.

The *Venetians* ioyned themselues with the *Frenchmen* against the state of *Millaine*,[21] which they needed not to haue doon, and as ytt chaunced afterwarde they felte the smart of it and with their owne losse payed the pryse of their rashnes. But yf necessitie enforce a prince to inclyne to one syde, which was the case of the *Florentynes* when the pope and the kinge of *Spayne* invaded *Lumberdy*, then is he to be excused by the reasons before alleaged, lett noe man be perswaded [22] that he can take soe sure a councell in those cases, that he cannot be controlled, but rather thincke that he may be deceaved, for soe variable is the coorse of worldlie affaires, that the more a man seekes to escape one dainger, the lyker he is to fall into an other, but herein is a mans wisdome seene, yf he be able of twoe evilles to choose the least, and can reape some commodity owt of anie inconvenience.

Besydes this a prince should indeavour to be thought a lover of vertues, and shoulde esteme those highly that excell in anie scyence. Moreover he should encorrage his Citizens and other subiectes, that they maye hope peaceably and quietlie to followe their trade, whether it be in merchandize

[f42] or in tillage,[28] or in any other trade, least the one sorte
for feare of spoylinge should leave the grownde vntilled
and the other in dowbte of newe exactions and customes,
shoulde bringe in noe [24] newe wares: But rather a good prince
shoulde propose [25] rewardes to those that dilligentlie followe
these trades, or anie other, whereby the Cittyes or contry
may be enriched. Alsoe att the appoynted tymes of the yeare
lett him keape the peoples heades occupyed with playes, and
shewes. And whereas the Cittyes are devided into certeine
Companies accordinge to their trades, and occupacions, the
prince shoulde haue those companies in estimation and rek-
oninge, that [26] shoulde soomtyme be conversante emonge
them, and shewe them soome token of his Courtesy and
favour. Provided alwayes that he preserve and still mayntaine the maiestie of his estate, which in noe wise, or anie
cause [27] ought to be omittted or neglected.

Of those that are councellours to princes. Cap: 22.

THE skilfull and advised Iudgmente of a prince in the
choyse of his Servauntes and officers, is a matter of noe
small importance seinge by their election men iudge of his
discreation, for the cheefest coniecture that is made of a
princes disposition, is taken by observinge the condicions
of those that are conversante abowt him, and yf they be
skilfull in their knowledge,[1] and faythfull in their councell,
he must needes be thought discreet, that coulde soe well
iudge of their sufficiencie, and soe wislie continewe their
secresie, but yf men thincke hardlie of them, it is not lyke
that they will thincke well of him, for the fowlest faulte
that a Prince can committ is in the badd choyse of these
kynde of men.

There was noe man that knewe *Antonius Venafrus*, serv-
ant to Pandolphus Petruccius, Prince of *Siena*, which did not
accompte *Pandolphus* a man of singuler wisdome for keepinge such a councell[2] abowte him. Ffor seinge mens wis-
domes and Capassities are of three[3] sortes, one sufficient of
it self[4] to descerne and iudge of causes. An[5] other hable[6]
to continewe and followe the advise that is geeven[7] itt, and
the last[8] that knowes nothinge it self, nor will learne of
other men. The[9] fyrst exell*es* aboue the reste and the seconde
is not muche inferiour to itt, but the thirde is altogether
vnproffitable, it must needes followe that the wisdom and
discretion of *Pandolphus* must be reckoned, (yf not in the
first) yet sure in the seconde degree, soe longe as a prince
is hable of himself to iudge of those thinges which are doon
or spoken before him, though he be not of that dexteritie to
invent or devise them: yet shall he quicklie perceaue whether
they be well concluded of by his councell, and may allowe
of this, and[10] disallowe of that att his pleasure, and his officers
perceavinge that he cannot lyghtlie be[11] deceaved will
hardlie fall from their dutie and[12] allegeau*n*ce.

Nowe to knowe the wisdome and disposition of a coun-
cello*ur*, this is an infallible rule, when thow fyndest him to
be more greedy of his owne gayne, then carefull of thy
co*m*moditie, in all his actions respectinge his owne proffitt,
thowe mayest[13] be sure he will never prove good councel-
lo*ur* nor such a one in whom thowe mayest repose anie
confidence, for he that hath the managinge of the affayres of
an other mans wealthe in his hand*es* shoulde never thincke
on his owne case, but his princes co*m*moditie, nor beate his
braines to augment his owne tryfles, but to increase his
princ*es* treasure. Againe it is the parte of a prince the better[14]
to keepe such a servaunte in dutie and allegeau*n*ce, to
thincke vppon him that takes payne for his proffitt, and to

rewarde him with honour and wealthe and variety of offices, that havinge those thinges heaped on him by his owne *Master* he neede not seeke it by any other meanes and that feelinge the sweetnes of those guyftes and prefermentes, he shoulde feare alteracion, knowinge that his state dependes on his princes safetie, for that newe chainge of kynges bringes newe choyse of Councellours.

When the Prince and his councellour be thus affected they maie boldely putt confidence the one in the other, but beinge otherwise mynded it is greate chaunce but one of them comes to a miserable ende.

[f43]

Howe to auoyde Flatterrers. Cap: 23.

I CANNOT overslippe one faulte and common errour which fewe princes may not be toucht withall, vnlesse they be indued with an excellent wytte to espye [1] the frawde, and with deepe iudgmente to make choyce of their frendes, that is geevinge eare to flatterrers. Ffor the avoydinge [2] whereof, all historyes are full of preceptes: but men are soe drowned in their conceiptes that they cannot be drawen, to shunn their Conference: and soe bewitched with their pleasinge talke, that they cannot beware the poyson of their tonges, and in avoydinge this inconvenience there is greate dainger lest he fall into contempte, for there is noe better waye for a prince to deliver himself from the mischeeffe of fflatterrers, [3] then to geeue men leave to speake their myndes freelie. And [4] yf men haue that libertie to speake what they please, they will quicklie deminishe the reputacion of the Prince. Therefore a wise prince should take a therd waye and make choyse of

some speciall men within his Dominion that haue good iudgment of matters of state, and make it onlie lawfull for them
to speake it vntrobled, when their opinions shalbe required,
and not before, neither pressinge into [5] Councell before they
be calde, nor settinge downe their opinion before the question be proposed.[6]

Yet shoulde the Prince demaunde of everie one of them
their opinions, and heare theyr iudgment*es* and ditermyne
with himself afterward whether of their councell*es* he
meanes to followe, and soe behave himself toward*es* them all
that they may perceave that he is allowed best, that speakes
his mynde boldest[7] and that he will not geeue eare to anie
other that shall contrarie the determination that was concluded emongst them, nor suffer himself by anie meanes to
be drawen from his purposed resolluc*i*on, he that doth otherwise shall either fall into the hand*es* of Flatterrers, or by the
contrariety[8] of opinions be driven continewallie from his
determination, and soe in the ende be coumpted vnconstante,
which will quicklie[9] impeache the estimation of his hono*ur*,
for prooffe whereof, I will recyte an example that is yet
freshe in memory. *Lucas* a Preest servaunte to *Maximilian*
that is nowe Empero*ur* talkinge[10] of his *Master*, sayde, that
he tooke councell of noe man, nor brought to passe anie
thinge he desyred,[11] which chaunced because he did take
a cleane contrarie coorse to that which wee haue prescribed.
Ffor the Empero*ur* is verie secret to himself communicatinge
his affayres to noe[12] man, nor callinge anie to councell in
his matters of State, but as soone as they are revealed, to be
putt in execution they are strayte contraried by those that
are abowte him, and he beinge affable by nature, and reddy
to be ledd, is straight altered from his former resoluc*i*on, by
this[13] meanes that which is doon one[14] daie is vndoon the
next[15] because noe man knowes his drifft nor can ayme at

his devise, or bylde anie certeintie [16] vppon his determinacions. Wherefore a prince should take councell in all his affaires, and yet not be tyed to heare it when other men lyke [17] to geeue it, but when he doth lyke to aske it; but should rather make them affrayde to offer to geeue their advise in anie matter before their councell were required, but lett him consulte often, and be content with pacience to heare the truthe spoken in those cases, which it hathe pleased him to propose emongst them, and to take the matter in verie evill parte yf anie man conceale it for anie private respect.

There are manie that thincke that a prince that is accompted wise hath not raysed that opinion of him self by [18] anie deserte or perfection of his owne nature, but by followinge the devise [19] of such discreete councellours as are abowte him: but they are all deceaved, for this is an infallible rule, that a prince that is not wise of him self, cann never take good councell of an other, it may [20] fall owte otherwise by chaunce, or greate fortune in a prince that hath geeven himself over to be ruled altogether by one man, for he may be governed well for the tyme, but it cannott longe endure, but his [21] tutour wilbe soe bolde in the ende, as to sett him asyde the cusshion, and take the place himself. Nowe yf a prince that wanteth discreation him self, will take this course to be governed by the direction of many, itt cannot be chosen but as they [22] be manie men, soe they must haue manie myndes, and they differringe in their [f44] opinions, and he neither hable to reconsyle them in one nor make choyse of the best, is lyke to take small proffitt by their councell, as for them they will looke everie man to his owne proffitte and neglectinge his safetie shyfte for their owne selues which because he cannot knowe, he cannot tell howe to correcte. Better fruyct then this noe man can hope for at theyr handes, for men are naturallie geeven to be vicious

and proane [28] to doe ill, yf they be not constrayned to be
verteous and provoked to doe well. Wherefore I conclude
that councell is made good by the wisdom of the prince, but
not the prince wise by the goodnes of the Councell.

What was the cause that certeine Princes of Italie
*   haue loste their estates.*   *Cap:* 24.

A PRINCE that by frende*s* or fortune or anie other meanes
   is newly raysed to the glorie of his dignitie, but [1] observinge wisly the precept*es* before prescribed shall seeme as
though he came by the estate [2] by anciente inheritau*n*ce, and
maye presentlie provide as good meanes for his safetie and
continuaunce, as yf he had spente all his tyme in the govermente of the contry, for men observe with greater regarde
the proceedinges of such princes, then of those that succeede
their parent*es* [3] in their kingdomes, and yf they haue as good
skill to governe, as to gett, they may winne the heartes of
the People sooner by desertes and pleasure, then the other
by discentes and pedegrees, and continve their loves longer
by the authoritie of their lawes, then the other can doe by the
antiquitie of their lynes,[4] for men are carried awaye rather
with thing*es* that are presente, then with those that are paste,
and fyndinge in it a co*m*moditie, they content them selues
and seeke noe farther, but will vndertake anie daynger in
defence of their princes saftie, soe such a prince shall gayne
to himself duble hono*u*r, aswell because he was the
Fownder of a newe principality, as alsoe for establishinge
therein good lawes for peace, and good discipline for warr,
and providinge good Armes for their defence and good
ffrende*s* to take their parte, and soe lykwise shall he incurr
dooble ignominie, that beinge a prince by birthe falles from

his estate for wante of goverment and becomes a private
man to his woonderfull greeffe. Nowe yf there be anie that
will consider of these [5] princes of *Italye* that in *our* dayes
haue fallen from their highe estates, as for example the kinge
of *Naples,* the duke of *Millaine* and such others, they shall
fynde in them all the generall defecte in providing [6] sufficient
armes for their defence, that we haue mentioned before, and
moreover shall see that manie of them were hated of their
Comunaltie, or yf they had their goodwilles they knew not
howe to bridle the ambition of the nobilitie, for those States [7]
and principalityes that are of sufficient power to bringe an
armye of their owne soldiers into the feelde can never be
overthrowne withowte some greate oversighte. *Phillip* of
Macedone (not the ffather of *Alexander* the greate but he
that was vanquished by *T: Quintus,*) had but a small kingdome in comparison of the *Romans* & *Grecians* that did invade him. Yet beinge a man of a warlike disposition, and by
experience made skilfull in all martiall stratagems, knowinge
both howe to wynne the heartes of the Comon people, and
alsoe to keepe the nobilitie within the bowndes [8] of their
dutie, was able to make warres with them manie Yeares, and
thoughe [9] he loste some of his Citties to them, yet he alwaies
kepte his kingdom to him self. Wherefore these *Italian
princes* of *our* tyme, that helde their state manie yeares by
succession, are not to blame fortune for the losse of their
segnioryes, but their owne negligence had provided not better for their [10] safeties. For [11] seinge in tyme of peace they
never thought vppon chaynge (which is a common fawlte
emonge men, never to thincke vppon a storme soe longe as
the wether is calme) when trowbles did ryse they never
trowbled their braines to defende their liberties by force, but
shamefully turned their backes to save their lyves by flighte,
hopinge that the people weried [12] and impatiente of the Con-

quero*urs* insolencie, woulde call them backe in the [f45] ende to their former dignitie, w*h*ich is a good mynde when there is non other meanes. But itt is a greate shame to neglect all other good help*es*, onlie in respect of this vncerteine hope,[13] for noe man shoulde be soe foollishe to fall[14] in hope to fynde others that wilbe readie to rayse him. For that[15] chaunces[16] seldom in princes causes:[17] or yf[18] it doe, the prince that is soe restored by other mens force, shall live[19] in his estate continewally in feare. For[20] those defences are surest and will stande thee best in steede that proceed*es* from thy self and from thy vertue, not from thy subiectes and their valure.

Of what power fortune is in Worldly affayres and the meane to withstande it. *Cap: 2 5.*

I AM NOT yet ignorante that manie haue ben & presentlie are of opinion that the dispensation of worldlie matters doth hange in such sort vpon god & fortune, that yt ys utterly impossible by[1] anie humane pollicye to disappoynte it. And therefore it might be thought bootlesse to be overcarefull or curiouse in those causes, but to[2] yeelde in such poynt*es* to the courtezie of Fortune. This opinion hath ben more easilie enterteined in *our* tyme, because of the manifolde changes of thing*es*. And[3] for that there haue ben alteracions seen,[4] (and daylie are seen) quyte beyonde the compasse of all humane coniecture, w*h*ich when I had oftentymes debated in my mynde, I fell in some parte to imbrase the same opinion. And yet least the power of *our* owne freewill shoulde seeme altogether voyde and frustrate, I am of this opinion that one parte of *our* affaires is disposed att the pleasure of For-tune,[5] and the other parte or little lesse to be lefte att the libertie of *our* owne discreation: for I maie compare fortune to a mountaine flood that beat*es* downe all before it, w*h*ich when it falles downe hedlonge overflowes the feeld*es*, break*es* vpp trees, and destroyes houses, in one place tearinge vpp a greate masse of earth,[6] and castinge it on an other. It mak*es* havocke of all before it, everie thinge feares it, and geeves place to the furie thereof, w*i*thowt anie meane or possibility to asswage it: Notw*i*thstandinge although it be somtymes carried w*i*th such violence, yet in calmer tydes may men provide w*i*th da*m*mes banck*es* pyles and such lyke, that att the nexte invndac*i*on it shall fall downe the right channell*es* and followe the ordinarie coorse or at the leastwise represse the fury of it in such sorte that it shall neither soe farr nor daingerouslie overflowe[7] the bowndes. The lyke falles owte in fortune w*h*ich then chefflie declares her power, when there is noe preparac*i*on for force to resist her,[8] and thither bend*es* all her furie where shee knowes there are noe bulwoork*es* nor stopp*es* to w*i*thstande her. And nowe yf a man looke into the state of *Italye*, the verie lodge and dwellinge place of these alterac*i*ons, w*h*ich hath raysed vpp these trowbles and tempest*es* he shall easilie perceave it to be as a waste and desert lande w*i*thowt either fortresse or fence, w*h*ich yf it had ben supported w*i*th necessarie vertue and valure of the Inhabitant*es*, as wee see *Germany, Spayne,* & *Fraunce*, this inundac*i*on had never broken into it, nor the contrie had runn a floate w*i*th such disordred alterac*i*ons as it did. And soe lett this suffyse as[9] the meane to w*i*thstande fortune. But to speake more neerely of the speciall poynt*es*, I say that any prince maye for this daye seeme to floorish in all shewe of happynes, to morrowe fall hedlonge into a thousande inconveniences, when to our thinckinge neverthelesse there is noe chainge either in his mynde or disposition.

Which I suppose principallie to proceede from the causes

before specified, syth wee see by common experience, that
the prince which surely [10] dependes vppon the onlie favour
and grace of fortune, dothe commonlie fall into vtter ruyne
when fortune chaingeth her coppye.

Againe I thincke him a fortunate Prince whose Councelles
and pollicyes of govermente are answerable to the state
of the tyme. On the other syde, I accompte him vnfortunate
that fyndes the tymes runn contrarie to the course of his
proceedinges, for it is a manifest experimente that all men followe not lyke councelles to [f46] hitt the marke whereatt
they levell, as renowme royallties, and such lyke, which
they haue ever before their Eyes as the stopp & drifte of all
their Actions. Some attempte it discreetly and with sownde
deliberacion, others rashlie vppon a sodaine braynesicke
moode, manie with force, some with pollicie, some by in-
duraunce and patience, others with an vnbridled heate without advise or anie deliberacion, and yet it is possible that
everie one of these may in the ende compasse the effecte of
their purposes, although the manner of their proceedinges
haue ben cleane different one from an other; Againe where
twoe men affect one driffte, wee shall see the one [11] that
vseth discreation [12] in his actions to atteine his desyre, and
the other to fayle his purpose, and yet shall wee see other
twoe attayne lyke good successe although their devises were
cleane contrary in execution, all which is caused of nothing
elles but the states [13] of tymes which doe either further or
crosse the manner of their Actions. And herevppon it falles
owt as I haue sayde, that twoe men attemptinge anie thinge
by divers councelles,[14] gayne notwithstanding a full and
equall effect of both their purposes; lykewise other twoe [15]
laboringe the same intente, the one bringes itt to passe the
other fayles: Hence alsoe proceedeth the interchaingable
coorse of good which falles owte soe common in the admin-

istracion of humane matters; for yf anie man in the govermente of his affaires beare himself circumspectly with a
setled mynde alwayes framinge his Actions and indeavours
to the state of the tymes, there is noe dowbte but his purpose
shall prosper, but yf the tymes and state of matters chaynge,
and crosse [16] the administration of his affayres, then all is
marred because with the chainge of tyme he alterred not the
maner of his devises.[17] And yet it is hard to fynde a man of
such wisdome, that knowes howe to conforme himself to
the nature of the tymes, aswell for that he will hardlie forgoe
that course wherevnto nature drawes him, as alsoe for that
he cannot be easily perswaded to forsake that direction
wherein heretofore he hath alwaies prospered. And therefore
he that deales with deliberacion and advise whille tyme
serves cann never be brought to runn headlonge or rashlie
abowte his Actions, and hence comes his vndooinge, where
otherwise yf he had alterred his nature and applyed itt to
the quallities of the tymes, his olde good fortune had never
fayled him. *Pope Iulius* [18] the seconde of that name was
passinge braynsycke and heady in everie thinge he wente
abowt, but he fownde the tymes, and state [19] of thinges soe
consonante to the nature of his Actions, that evermore he
broughte his devises to a prosperous effecte. Doe but marke
and consider his first enterprise in the *Bononian* expedition.
John Bentiuoli Prince of the Citty, was then livinge. The
Venetians tooke the matter in verie evill [20] parte. The kinges
of *Spayne*, & *Fraunce*, entred into devise against it. He notwithstandinge with the same heate he began proceeded
rowndly in person to the execution of his purpose, with
which harebraynde resollucion he caste the *Spaniards* and
Venetians in such a quandarie,[21] that he kepte them bothe in
mere awe, the one parte with feare the other with hope to
recover the wholle kingdom of *Naples*. On the other syde

he drewe the french kinge to his ayde and assistaunce, whoe seinge him soe readie and prest for Armes, and withall desiringe his amity to the ende he might more safelie invade the *Venetians*, thought he shoulde doe him manifest iniurie in denyinge to ayde him with his Armyes and so *Iulius* by feersnes, and secure resollucion brought that to passe which never anie other of the Bishoppes were hable to atchive by anie humane pollicie whatsoever. For[22] had he protracted anie daies before his settinge foorth of *Rome* till all thinges had ben determined and concluded with[28] longe and orderlie deliberacion (as anie other Bishope in the lyke case woulde haue thought best) he had fayled all the fortunate successe of that expedicion. For the *Frenche* kinge wolde haue forged and fayned a thousand devises to linger the purpose, and drawe backewarde, the other woulde [f47] haue daynted[24] and discoorraged hym[25] wellnere with infinite terrours. I omitt the rest of his actes, which resemblinge this, for the most parte in execution and successe, arrived alsoe to the marke and ende of his desyre. But the shortnes of his Lyffe prevented all fortunes which might fall owte contrarie to the firste. For[26] yf he had chaunced vppon those tymes, as were to crave carfull deliberacion, and soom advise, his distruction must needes haue followed, because he coulde never be perswaded from that sodaine braynsicke disposition wherevnto he was inclyned by nature. Lett this therefore stande for an infallible rule[27] that men shall alwaies fynde fortunate successe, yf they frame and fashion the state and course of their affaires accordinge to the turnes and alteracions of fortune. But contrariwise striving against fortune they come to extreame miserie & Ruyn. Ffor fortune is a wooman, and he that will raigne over her, must of force be fayne both to maister her, and quicken her with a Cudgell. And all men see shee yeeldeth more willinglie to them that vse her roughlie and severelie then to those that intreate her coldlie and fayntelie. And therefore in respect she is a wooman wee prove her by experience more gratious and favorable to younge men, for commonly they haue leaste regarde, and are soe resollut to all attempt*es* that they overmaster fortune her self, with valure and Coorrage.

An exhortation to deliver *Italye* from the *Barbarians*. *Cap:* 26.[1]

WHEREFORE in consideration of all causes before specified [2] casting in my mynde whether the present state of *Italye* vnder the conduct of anie newe prince lately raysed to honor [3] might by the goverment of anie verteous and wise man be ordred in such sorte,[4] as might bee both for his hono*ur* and the benefitt of all *Italy*. Such soondrie comodities and oportunities presented themselves to my Iudgmente,[5] that I cannot possibly imagine a fitter tyme then this present for the purpose. Ffor as wee haue sayde before to make the vertue of *Moyses* more famous, it was necessarie that the *Israllytes* shoulde suffer captivitie in *Egipte*, and to make the greatenes of *Cyrus* renowme, that the *Persians* shoulde be opprest by [6] the *Medes*, and soe in lyke sorte to illustrate the magnificence of *Theseus*, the wandringe and dispersed state [7] of the *Athenians* was to great purpose. Soe att this tyme for declaracion of anie sparke of the *Italians* valour, it was first requisite that Italie shoulde be brought to those miserable extremities wherein it standes [8] att this present. And to be yoked in more thrall then the *Hebrues*, in more tiranous slaverye then the *Persians*, to be disperst and scatterred farther asoonder then the *Athenians* withoute guyde or govermente scourged with whipp*es*, spoylde of their good*es*, seuered one from an other, everie where bayted and turmoyled with everie kynde of calamitie. And although the man hath lived and floorished [9] in those *our* dayes that hath partlie promised some hope of that coorrage,[10] whereby wee might iudge him to be destitute of [11] god himself, for the delivery of *Italye*. Notwithstandinge it fell owte in the prooffe of his proceedinges that fortune abandoned him in such sorte that he laye as a man withowt Lyffe, lookinge for an other to heale his woundes and to ende the spoyles, fyres, and wastes of *Lumbardy*, and to ceasse the pillage tributes and intollerable impositions both of *Naples*, and *Tuscanes*, and to cure those sores which by longe continewaunce are growne well nere incureable. And nowe wee see the Contrie of *Italye* it self, prayinge to almightie god for one other to deliver it from the presente tiranye and insolencie of the *Barbarians*. Wee see alsoe howe proane and readye shee is to followe anie standerd or baner that makes prooffe of her freedom. Neither att this tyme dothe the Contrie see any better guyde or aucthor [12] of her redemption [f48] then the famous house of the *Medices*, beinge glorious aswell by private vertues, and prosperous fortune, as favored by God him self and honour of the ecclesiasticall govermente, wherein att this tyme itt possesseth the soveraigne Principalitie.[18] Neither shall itt fynde anie greate difficultie in the matter, yf the Actes and maner of lyffe be considered of those famous men, whom wee haue before mencioned. And although they were rare and renowmed with all vertues, yett were they but mortall, and never had soe fitt oportunitie offerred them as wee haue att this presente for *Italie*. Ffor the notable enterprises they attempted were neither [14] more lawfull nor easie then this of owres; neither did God ever shewe himself more lovinge to them then to vs. And moreover in this there standethe singuler Iustice, for that waye [15] is iuste and righteous which

is necessarie, and those armes savo*ur* of pietie, where the generall hope consistethe in noe other meane [16] but in them, and
herein is passinge easye disposition of matters, wherein can
never anie greate difficultie arise. Yf the institution and forme
of Goverment be derived from those men, whom wee haue
sett downe, as the vearie drifte and marke whereatt wee
ayme. And furthermore for easier accomplishment for [17]
this purpose, there are manie vnaccustomed sygnes of the
favo*ur* of god exhibited vnto vs. The waye through the sea
lyes open, the Clowde hath offerred to be o*ur* guyde, the
rocke [18] hath powred owte Water, manna hath rayned from
heaven, and althinges concurr [19] to the increase of thy fam-
ilies renowme. The execution of the rest belonges to thy
house. God [20] doth not all by himself; for deprivinge vs of
all abillitie, neither doth he take that part of the glory w*h*ich
belonges to o*ur* share. Neither is anie man to mervayll yf noe
Italian pere before mencioned, could ever bringe that to
passe, w*h*ich maybe presentlie hoped of thy noble familye,
althoughe in soe manie alteracions of *Italye* and martiall
occurrences, the woonted [21] militarie vertue thereof seeme
well neere extinguished.[22] The reasons thereof beinge for
that the olde orders and institutions of martiall disciplyne
fitted not those tymes, neither did anie synce [23] springe vpp
w*h*ich knewe to invente anie newe in their steede. There is
nothinge that will [24] purchase a man more fame, that newly
aspyreth to hono*ur*, then the constitucion of newe lawes and
invention of newe orders for military affayres; for these
matters beinge sowndlie stablishte and bearinge shewe of
a certeine speciall excellencie, make the person to appeere
famous, and admirable to the Worlde. And in *Italie* there
wanteth noe possibilitie to bringe in anie newe forme of
lyffe whatsoever. And for the effectinge of these affaires
there woulde prove singuler valoure in the members, yf it

lacked not in those that shoulde be the head*es*. In single com-
bates and encounters att Armes, maybe seene as in a glasse
howe farr the *Italians* excell all other nations in strengthe
and agillitie of bodye, and valure of mynde. And yet when
they shoulde come foorthe to open battell, they are not to
be fownde. But all that [25] proceed*es* from the weaknes of
their head*es* and governours, for they that are skilfull indeede, them noe man obeyethe, because everie man
thincketh [26] himself sufficiente*ly* seenn in the practise of all
thing*es*, neither haue wee seen any man heretofore w*h*ich
by his vertue and good fortune hath aspyred to that greatnes
and aucthority, as to co*m*maunde all the rest. And herevppon
it came to passe, that in all this processe of tyme, in soe manie
warres managed these twentie yeares paste, there was [f49]
never anie feelde froughte, but the Armye was in extreame
daynger of vtter losse and overthrowe, yf itt consisted
wholly of *Italians*. And first for witnes hereof, looke into
the battell foughte att the River of *Tarro*, then att *Alexandria*,[27] *Genua, Capua, Vuila, Bononia*, and *Mestria*. And
therefore yf thy famous and honorable house intende [28] to
followe the examples [29] of these woorthy men, w*h*ich sett
their contries att libertie, it must thincke this necessarie before all thinges (as a Principall fowndac*i*on) to be provided
of proper and Domesticall Warfarre.

Ffor there is noe man can possibly hope to fynde anie more
trustie, more sure and fytt, then those of thy [30] owne makinge. And although they be severallie good, yet shall they
bee better when they are ioyned all in one, and haue their
owne naturall prince to co*m*maunde them, and to fight as
well for his owne hono*ur* as for their safetie.

And therefore [31] to defende him self from foraine invasions itt shalbe verie necessarie to provide him self furnished
of such aydes, and although the *Swisers* and *Spanishe* Foot-

men seeme terrible to manie, yet are they not awnswerable in every respecte.[32] And therefore yf anie man coulde devise a middle order of battell, there were good hope not onlie to withstande, but alsoe to overcom them.

The *Spaniardes* cannot beware the shocke of the men att armes, and the *Swisers* haue woorke enough to encounter the footemen of their Enemyes, which are as readie and resollute as themselues, wherein wee haue seene by experience (and shall hereafter fynde itt trewe by prooffe) that the *Spaniardes* haue ben foyled by the *french horsmen* and the *Swysers* by the *Spanishe footemen*, and althoughe the example hath not generallie helde att this last deede doon, yet haue wee seen an evident signe in the Battell of *Rauenna*, where the *Spaniardes* and *Germanes* fought a sett Battell of Footmen, both vsinge the same order of fyghte as the *Swisers*, where the *Spanishe bandes* beinge nimbler of bodye and defended with their targettes brake into the mayne battell and gettinge within the longe vnweldy Pykes of their Enemyes, spoyled and mangled them att pleasure withowte rescue or resistaunce the *Germans* were able to make. And had not the troopes of horssmen geeven a hoatt charge vppon them, they had putt everie man to [33] the swoorde. And therefore a newe forme of militarie discipline might be devised nowe that bothe these nations haue discovered eche others defectes, and that newe manner of service shoulde be such, as bothe might beare the charge of men att armes, and never neede to feare the Footemen. And yet is not that to be doon with chainge of Armes or wepons but by alteracion of anciente orders.

And this [34] devise may be reckoned emonge those which beinge newlie ordeyned and established, purchasse greate reputacion and honour to a newe prince. Wherefore this opportunitie is not to be lett slypp owte of our handes, by execution whereof poore *Italy* mighte beholde her longe wished redemer. Neither can I easilie expresse,[85] with what loue, with what pantinge thirst of revenge, with what assuraunce, with what cincerity of mynde, with what abundance of teares those provinces woulde entertaine theire Redemer after soe longe oppression of Forreyne Rabbles. What Gates shoulde be shutt against him? what sorte of People would refuse to obey him? what envie woulde withstande him? what one man of the Italian Nation woulde refuse to followe him. There is none I saie there is none that doth not loathe & abhour this beastlie kynde of Principalitie.

Lett thie noble family attempte this honorable enterprise with that mynde and that hope as all Iuste actions [f50] are taken in hande. That vnder their Ensignes this Contry maybe renowmed, and by the grace of their good fortune the sayinge of *Petrarke* maybe verified.

That Valiante men shall beare corragious Armes
againste barbarous force, and rowndlie play their partes,
For ancient Valure (mauger all their harmes)
is not yet dead in braue Italian heartes.[36]

NOTES

Of Liberalitie and sparing / Cap: 16

Lower part of folio 27v
Furthman Manuscript

NOTES

I<small>N THE</small> following notes the Harley manuscripts at the British Museum which contain English translations of Machiavelli's *Il Principe* are referred to as H. 6795, H. 967, and H. 364; Ashmole MS 792 at the Bodleian Library, as A. 792; the manuscript translation belonging to Mr. Jules Furthman (which forms the basis of the text here printed), as MS. Ital. denotes the Italian text, which has been drawn from *Il principe di Niccolò Machiavelli: Testo critico . . . a cura di Giuseppe Lisio (Firenze, 1899), with variant readings there supplied. Fr. denotes the French translation of Jacques Gohorry (*Le Prince de Nicolas Machiavelli secretaire et citoyen florentin. . . . Traduit d'Italien en François avec le vie de l'auteur mesme, par Iaq. Gohory Parisien*, Paris, 1571). The Latin translation of Sylvester Telius is referred to as Lat. The usual reference is to the first edition, *Nicolai Machiavelli Reip. Florentinæ a secretis, ad Laurentium Medicem de Principe libellus*. Basileæ apud Petrum Pernam. M.D.LX.

DEDICATORY LETTER

The Dedicatory Letter, here set in italic, is in secretary hand in MS.

1. price. H. 967, *prize;* A. 792, *greatest price;* H. 6795 defective.

2. Ffor. ff is used by the writer of MS both for capitals and small letters. When this character stands for a capital it has been reproduced as in *Ffor.* The capitalization of MS has been followed except where noted. Most capitals occurring in the text are for emphasis, although it is to be suspected that in certain cases, particularly C and E, the copyist habitually used the capital form.

3. some. Written here, and usually below, with a line over o. The same is true of *come* and some other words spelled with a single nasal consonant. Except in cases where this mark indicates an omitted m or n it has been disregarded.

4. thanck*es.* Final *-es* in *thanck*es represents the scribal sign for the plural. Since -es seems to be the normal spelling of the scribes, the scribal sign has been given as *-es* except in a few cases where the usage seems to be in favor of *s.*

5. actes councells and governments. A. 792 and H. 967, which are slightly more modern in punctuation than MS and H. 6795, place a comma after *actes.* The punctuation of MS has been allowed to stand except in cases in which the weight of manuscript authority seems to be against it.

6. intermeddle. H. 967, which shows somewhat greater

freedom in language than MS, has *medle*. Such variations are ordinarily not recorded.

TABLE OF CHAPTERS

1. Howe Citties ... libertye. Fr., *Comme on doibt gouer-
   ner les citez ou principautez lesquelles auant qu'elles
   fussent conquises uiuoyent à leur loix;* Lat., which
   seems much closer to MS, *Quomodo civitates, aut prin-
   cipatus regi debeant, qui suis legibus & libertate uiue-
   bant.*

CHAPTER I

1. *These.* The t in *These*, though a small letter, is larger
   than usual; so often below.

CHAPTER II

1. *this.* H. 6795 has *thus*, a way of writing the word which
   frequently recurs in that manuscript.

2. *vsurper.* H. 967, *disturber.*

3. *1516* [*1510*]. The event referred to occurred in 1510,
   and the date is correctly given in Ital., Fr., and Lat., yet
   all copies of the English version have 1516.

4. *cleere rased.* So H. 6795; H. 967, *will cleerly be raised;*
   A. 792, *cleene razed.* Agreement between MS and H.
   6795 is usually to be regarded as determinative of the
   original text.

CHAPTER III

1. *But in ... mixte.* This sentence affords a clear indication of the use of the Latin version of Telius, which

reads, *Sed in eo qui recens accessit principatu, difficultates continentur, tum maximè, si veluti pars adiuncta
(ut sic in universum mixtus dici possit) non penitus est
nouus.* Ital. has, *Ma nel principato nuovo consistono le
difficultà. E prima, se non è tutto nuovo, ma come membro, che si può chiamare tutto insieme quasi misto, le
variazioni sua nascono in prima da una naturale difficultà, la quale è in tutti e'principati nuovi.* Fr. renders
Ital. Our version translates the unique expression of Lat.,
se veluti pars adiuncta, in logical terminology, *as a parte
adjoyned.* H. 6795, *as parte;* H. 967, *a parte;* A. 792
agrees with MS.

2. *they.* H. 6795 has *the,* as frequently below, for *they.*

3. *wherein.* So A. 792; H. 6795, *wherby.*

4. Sfortia. MS here uses the Latin form of the name as
against Ital. *Ludovico.*

5. *retayned.* MS shows *reclaymed* written and crossed out,
retayned written above it; H. 6795 has *withdrawne.*
It is significant in the grouping of the MSS that H. 967
follows MS, with *retained,* and A. 792 agrees with
H. 6795, with *withdrawen.*

6. *surely.* H. 6795, *suerly;* H. 967, *safely;* A. 792, *securelie.*

7. *the places.* MS and H. 6795 have *her places;* H. 967, *the
places.* The reading *her places* may be an attempt to ren-
der Lat., *sibi debiliora loca praemuniens.*

8. *must.* H. 6795, *must of necessity,* which is in agreement
with A. 792. H. 967 follows MS. In this case it would
seem that MS has the original form and that H. 6795 as
also A. 792, has repeated *of necessity* from the line
above.

9. *goverment.* This spelling of government is characteristic of all manuscripts, being especially frequent in MS and H. 6795.

10. *yf they be not.* So H. 967; H. 6795, *not yf they be,* which is also the reading of A. 792.

11. *extinguishe.* So. H. 967; H. 6795 and A. 792, *distinguishe.*

12. *province.* MS, *prince;* also H. 967; H. 6795 and A. 792 show *province,* the correct reading, as appears from the Latin version, of which the English is clearly a translation: *Verùm imperia, quum comparantur in prouincia, quae in lingua, moribus, institutis discrepat: hîc adsunt difficultates, hîc labores, hîc magna felicitate, summaque industria, quo retineantur opus est.*

13. *able to.* MS catchwords at bottom of fol. 4r, *hable to.*

14. *planted.* So H. 6795; A. 792 and H. 967, *placed.*

15. *intrude.* So H. 6795 and A. 792; MS, *intend,* followed by H. 967.

16. *rediest.* H. 6795, *readiest;* H. 967, *presentst.*

17. *Colonies.* MS has here and three lines below the singular reading, *Colonells,* which is followed by H. 967. H. 6795 has *Colonies,* representing Lat. *Coloniae,* Fr. *colonies,* and Ital. *colonie.* A. 792 has unfortunately omitted a long passage, *An other* to *advancemente* (see n. 53, below), so that it throws no light on the point.

18. *greate;* H. 967; H. 6795, *greater.*

19. *them.* H. 6795, *then,* a frequent miswriting in that manuscript.

20. *all.* In this and many other cases *ll* is crossed. Since there seems to be no significance in these flourishes they have not been recorded.

21. *Colonies.* At this point the peculiar spelling "colonells" disappears, as if the scribe of MS misread the word up to this point and then saw the correct reading.

22. *Therefore these ... beneficiall.* Opposite these lines a later hand (probably seventeenth century), hereafter designated as hand B, has written: [*Co*]*lonies profitable for a State.* On the probable date of the marginal hand see notes below.

23. *weker.* H. 6795 and 967, *weake.*

24. *devise meanes ... Province.* In the margin hand B, *See Polyb: li. 1° ... ene extremo.* A reference to the unfortunate experience of the Carthaginians with foreign and mercenary troops as recorded in the later chapters of Book I of *Histories*, may be intended.

25. *straynger.* So H. 967; H. 6795, *straungers.*

26. *As it is.* So H. 967; H. 6795, *As is.*

27. *The* Romaines ... *Colonies.* In the margin, hand B, *Example from the Romans.*

28. Achaians & Ætolians *were spared.* The error Archaians for Achaians (see also three lines below) appears both in MS and in H. 6795. H. 967 has corrected it to *Achaians.* Ital. has *Furono intrattenuti da loro li Achei e li Etoli;* Lat., *Achæi, atque Aetoli fuerunt ab eis seruati.* The rendering, *were spared,* of MS clearly follows Lat. Dacres has *entertained,* which is the rendering of all versions consulted except Lat. and the present.

29. *but hard ... cure.* Supplied from H. 6795; H. 967 agrees
with MS. The omitted words represent Lat., *sed cognitu
difficilem: progressu verò temporis non percepta nec
curata, facilem esse vt cognoscatur, at vt quis eam
sanet perdifficilem*, rather than Ital., *e difficile a conoscere, ma, nel progresso del tempo, non l'avendo in
principio conosciuta né medicata, diventa facile a
conoscere e difficile a curare.*

30. *& may ... good.* Supplied from H. 6795; H. 967 agrees
with MS; Lat., *æque bonum ac malum, & malum ꝫquè
ac bonum secum ferre potest;* Ital., *e può condurre seco
bene come male, e male come bene.*

31. *But to ... degressed.* Lat. seems to be the basis of this:
Verum redeat oratio vnde digressa est ad Galliam;
Ital. has simply, *Ma torniamo a Francia.*

32. *healde.* H. 6795, *had;* H. 967, *held.*

33. *this syde.* Both MS and H. 6795 have *thissyde;* Lat.,
Cisalpinæ Galliæ.

34. *putt.* H. 6795, *set;* H. 967, *put.*

35. *driven.* So H. 967; H. 6795, *faine.*

36. Genua *yelded ... amitye.* MS shows no punctuation
after *frendes* or after Bentiuoly. Instead of Faenza MS
has Facuza; H. 6795, *facuza;* H. 967, *Fauiza.* Lat. has,
*Genua cesserat. Florentini in eius amicitiam venerant,
Mantuanus, & Ferrariensis principes, Forumliuij do-
mina, Bentiuolus, Fauentiæ, Arimini, Pisauri, tum Ca-
mertium, & Traiani portus reguli, Lucenses item, Pisani,
Senenses: hi omnes obviam ei processerant, in eius
amicitia futuri;* Ital., *Genova cedé; Fiorentini li divento-*

*rono amici; Marchese di Mantova, Duca di Ferrara,
Bentivogli, Madonna di Furlí, Signore di Faenza, di
Pisaro, di Rimino, di Camerino, di Piombino, Lucchesi,
Pisani, Sanesi, ognuno se li fece incontro per essere suo
amico;* Fr., *Genuesse rendit,les Florentins luj deuindrent
amis. Le Marquis de Mantouë, le duc de Ferare, les
Bentignoles, Madam de Furli, les seigneurs de Fauance,
de Pesare, de Rimin, de Camerin, & de Plombin, les
Luquois, Pisans, Sienois, chacun vint au devant de luj,
pour estre à sa deuocion.* It is obvious in both MS and
H. 6795 that the writers have understood Bentiuoly
maddam of Furly as signifying one person, also that
those texts have both misread Faenza as Facusa; the
phrase, *the States of Mantua and Ferrara,* translates
more nearly the Latin, *Mantuanus, & Ferrariensis principes,* than it does the Italian or the French. In one expression, *maddam of* Furly, there may be evidence of
Gohorry's French translation, *Madam de Furli,* although the Italian *madonna di Furli* would have served
as well. To the expression, *all these enterteigned him
and desired his amitye,* the French is perhaps nearest.
The grammatical construction of the English is like that
of the Italian and the French.

37. *2 Cittyes.* H. 6795, *the;* H. 967, *twoe;* Lat., *duas in Cisalpina Gallia vrbes.*

38. *he dreaded.* H. 6795, *is dreaded;* H. 967, *he has dreaded;*
Lat., *ab illis, qui potentiores reliqui essent.*

39. *these.* So H. 967; H. 6795, *all these.*

40. Flaminia. It is difficult to see how this name could have
come into the text except from Lat., which translates

the Italian *Romagna* by the ancient name of the region. Fr. has *Romagne*.

41. *forecaste.* H. 6795 omits; H. 967, *forecast.*

42. *Empire.* H. 6795, *empirie*; so with *insolencie* for *insolence*, three lines below and with various other words of the kind.

43. *on.* H. 6795, *a*; H. 967 as usual agrees with MS.

44. *thirsted.* H. 6795, *thirst.*

45. *hable.* H. 967, *able*; H. 6795, *noble*; Lat., *modo possint*; Ital., *che possano.*

46. *five errours.* MS has no punctuation after *errours*; H. 6795 has comma. In the margin, hand B, *French King* [*fell*] *into five errors.*

47. *mightie.* H. 6795, *forrein*; Lat., *potentioris potentiam.*

48. *soe.* H. 6795, *also*; H. 967, *so.*

49. *warr.* MS has period after *warr*; H. 6795, no point.

50. *therebye.* H. 967, *theareby*; H. 6795, *hereby.*

51. *Nantes.* So H. 6795 and H. 967; MS, *Mantes.*

52. *did take.* So H. 967; H. 6795, *tooke.*

53. *advancemente.* End of omission in A. 792.

CHAPTER IV

1. *which.* H. 6795 omits; A. 792 and H. 967 agree with MS.

2. *it but.* MS places period after *it* and write *But*; text follows H. 6795.

3. *sundry kinde*s ... *most.* Supplied from H. 6795, with which A. 792 agrees; H. 967 follows MS in omitting these words; punctuation from H. 6795; MS has comma after *examples* and writes *the.*

4. *many.* So H. 967; H. 6795, *diuers*; A. 792, *sundrie.*

5. *and.* So A. 792 and H. 967; H. 6795, *or.*

6. *pleasure.* MS has no point after *pleasure* and writes *but.*

7. *myddes.* H. 6795, *mindes*; A. 792, *middest.*

8. *The reasons.* In margin, hand B, *Reason why the Turkish Empire is hard to be woon.*

9. *seeme.* H. 6795 and A. 792, *semeth.*

10. *But.* So H. 967; H. 6795 and A. 792, *for.*

11. *malcontente*s. H. 6795, *all contentes*; A. 792 and H. 967 agree with MS. In margin, hand B, *Malcontents desyer inovation.*

12. *passage.* So A. 792 and H. 967; H. 6795, *passinge.*

13. *mayne.* H. 6795, *many*; A. 792 and H. 967 agree with MS.

14. *alleaged.* MS places comma after *alleaged*, but writes *And.*

15. *ancient lyues.* Lat. *quam diu viguit.*

16. *other.* So H. 967; H. 6795 and A. 792, *others*; so frequently with this word.

CHAPTER V

1. *inhabitaunce.* H. 6795, *inhabitants*; A. 792 agrees with MS.

2. *into.* So H. 967; H. 6795 and A. 792, *in.*

3. *For.* MS, *for.*

CHAPTER VI

1. *And.* MS, *and.*

2. *perfection.* So A. 792; H. 6795, *perfections.*

3. *geetter.* MS, first e blotted and indistinct. H. 6795, *greater*; A. 792 and H. 967 agree with MS.

4. *we are not.* H. 6795, *we ar not heare*; A. 792 and H. 967 agree with MS.

5. *greatlie.* Top of f .'. ːc, hand B, *There must concurre both vertue and opportunity to doe any greate matter.*

6. *noble actes.* In the margin, hand B, *occasion fitting vertue.*

7. *And.* MS, *and*; H. 6795, *And.*

8. *Rome.* No point after this word in MS; H. 6795 and A. 792 have period and write *And.*

9. *Medes.* MS, *medes.*

10. *For.* MS, *for.*

11. *effecte.* So A. 792 and H. 967; H. 6795, *afecte.*

12. *or be.* So A. 792 and H. 967; H. 6795, *or to be.*

13. *Yf.* MS, *yf.*

14. *variable.* Margin, hand B, *Men naturally variable.*

15. *fayth.* H. 6795 omits this word; A. 792 and H. 967 agree with MS. Margin, hand B, *The lions skin must be had as well as the foxes.*

16. *such.* So H. 967; H. 6795 and A. 792, *this.*

17. *consistes.* So A. 792 and H. 967; H. 6795, *consisteth.*

18. Hieron. So. A. 792; H. 6795, *Hiero*; H. 967, *Hierom.*

19. *did wryte.* H. 6795 and A. 792, *wrote*; H. 967, *doe write.*

20. *He.* MS, *he.*

CHAPTER VII

1. *safetie.* H. 6795 places period after this word and writes *In*; A. 792 agrees with MS.

2. *tymes.* So H. 967; H. 6795 and A. 792, *tyme.*

3. *Segniories.* So A. 792; H. 6795, *Seigniorityes.*

4. *Things.* MS, *things*; so H. 6795.

5. *or florishe in such sort.* These words are introduced into the text from H. 6795; they appear also in A. 792, but not in H. 967; Lat., *nec radices agere, nec quæ eò respondeant habere possunt*; Ital. (variant from edition of Blado, 1532, appearing in Wolfe's edition, 1584), *non possono avere le radici e correspondentie loro in modo.*

6. *prince.* MS has period after this word; H. 6795, comma.

7. *yet.* MS has period after *atchived*; H. 6795, semicolon.

8. *provide.* So A. 792 and H. 967; H. 6795, *prevayle.*

9. Rome. MS places period after Rome.

10. Fauentia *and* Ariminum. So Lat.; Ital., *Faenza e Rimino.*

11. *might closely.* H. 6795 and A. 792, *closely might*; H. 967 as usual follows MS.

12. *sowe discorde.* In the margin, hand B, *divide et impera.*

13. *which.* So H. 967; H. 6795 and A. 792, *that.*

14. Romagnia. MS here and below has Italian form instead of Latin *Flaminia.*

15. *good.* So A. 792 and H. 967; H. 6795, *great.*

16. *the assaulte.* H. 6795, *thassault*, as often in such combinations.

17. Valentinus. In the margin, hand B, *Valentinus his practis.*

18. *inconstancie.* H. 6795 and A. 792, *vnconstancy.*

19. *forces.* MS has no punctuation after this word; H. 6795 has period and writes *Wherefore.*

20. Magio del Paragino. H. 6795, *Margiu*; A. 792, *Magio del Peragino.* Ital., *alla Magione, nel Perugino*; Lat., *Magione in agro Perusino*; Fr., *la Magion pres de Peruse.*

21. *reputation.* MS has no point after this word; H. 6795 and A. 792 have commas.

22. *apparrell ... mony.* H. 6795 and A. 792, *apparell, mony and horses*; H. 967 follows MS.

23. *insolencyes.* H. 6795, *Insolences.*

24. Remerus Orcus. H. 6795, *Remerus Orans*; H. 967 and A. 792 agree with MS.

25. *then.* H. 6795, *y^e*; A. 792, *the*; H. 967 follows MS.

26. *This.* MS, *this.*

27. *should.* So A. 792 and H. 967; H. 6795, *shall.*

28. *thereof.* H. 6795 omits; H. 967 and A. 792 agree with MS.

29. *Deputie.* In the margin, hand B, *Borgias pollecy to cast all the enuy of his owne cruelty vpon his Deputy.*

30. *humo*ur. So H. 967; H. 6795 and A. 792, *humours.*

31. *newe frendes.* In the margin, hand B, *his plotts.*

32. *successe.* In the margin, hand B, *see Guicc. lib. 4th.* The reference is to passages dealing with the Borgias canceled in the Latin and Italian editions of Guicciardini's *History.* These were added to Fenton's translation of Guicciardini in an edition published by Richard Field in 1618. As a later note shows, this is the edition of Guicciardini's *History* the annotator has in hand. The canceled passages had been printed in Basle (1561) and London (1595).

33. *affayres.* H. 6795 introduces *which* after this word; H. 967 and A. 792 agree with MS.

34. *fower wayes . . . feares.* In the margin, hand B, *He that offends neuer pardons.* On the margin below, at intervals, *meanes, meanes, meanes.*

35. *fowerthe.* No punctuation after this word in MS; H. 6795 has period.

36. [Piombino.] MS and H. 967 have a blank for this name. H. 6795 marks it with a verticle stroke; A. 792 has

remedied the defect by omitting *and*. Ital., *Piombino*;
Lat., *Traianus portus*.

37. *not, the Spaniardes*. MS, comma after *Spaniardes*, no
point after *not*.

38. Romagnia. No punctuation after Romagnia in MS.

39. *Armies*. After this word H. 6795 introduces, probably
as a repetition, *of twoe mighty princes;* A. 792 agrees
with MS.

40. *sicknes*. So H. 967 and A. 792; H. 6795, *successe*.

41. *This*. MS, *this*.

42. *And ... Baglians*. MS, *and ... baglians*.

43. *And*. MS, *and*.

44. *that*. H. 6795 and A. 792, *whom*; H. 967 follows MS.

44a. *carefullie forecast*. Marginal note, hand B, *Man pur-
poseth but god disposeth*.

45. *all*. H. 6795 and A. 792, *all the*; H. 967 follows MS.

46. *kyndes*. So H. 967 and A. 792; H. 6795, *kinde*.

47. *the seconde*. H. 6795 omits; A. 792 and H. 967 agree
with MS.

48. *yf*. H. 6795, *yf that*.

49. St. Peter ... Ascanius. All manuscripts seem to be confused. Ital. enumerates four: *San Piero ad Vincula, Co-
lonna, San Giorgio, Ascanio*; Lat. divides them into two
groups, *Quibus verò inter alios ipse inurium* [sic] *se
præstiterat Cardinalis Titulo diui Petri ad vincula erat,
& Columnius: Cardinalis item Titulo diui Georgij, &*

Ascanius. This odd grouping evidently gave rise to the confusion in the English version.

50. Rotoman*us.* This odd name for the Cardinal of Rouen arose apparently from Lat., *cum Rotomagensi cardinale.* The text is completely misunderstood in this passage. There is a period after Rotoman*us.* Ital. has *tutti li altri, devenuti papi, aveano a temerlo, eccetto Roano e li Spagnoli, questi per coniunzione et obligo, quello per potenzia, avendo coniunto seco el regno di Francia.* Lat. has the following confused construction: *cæteris omnibus id dignitatis fastigium assequutis timendus relinquebatur præter Rotomagensi, atqu*e *Hispanis: h*is *quide*m *ex officio, & sanguinis coni*u*nctione, illi verò propter potent*iam*, qu*ò*d esset Galliari*um *regi affinitate coni*u*nctus.* The French text, which is much abridged, refers to the cardinal as *Amboise.*

51. *bent.* H. 6795, *lent*; A. 792 agrees with MS.

Chapter VIII

1. *welthes.* MS and H. 6795, no punctuation after this word.

2. *discoursinge.* So H. 6795, H. 967, and A. 792; MS, *discoveringe.*

3. Agathocles. In the margin, hand B (?), *See Justine 22: Diodo. Siculus l: 20.* The basal references to the history of Agathocles the Tyrant are Justin, *Historiæ Philippicæ,* Bks. XXII and XXIII, and Diodorus Siculus, *Bibliotheca Historica,* Bks. XIX, XXI, and XXII.

4. *towardes.* H. 6795, *toward*; A. 792 agrees with MS.

5. *degresse.* Corrected to *degrees* in hand B.

6. *becom.* H. 6795, *be*; A. 792, *be come.*

7. *the Estate.* H. 6795 and A. 792, *there estate.*

8. *where.* Included within the parentheses in MS and in A. 792.

9. *doon.* So H. 967; H. 6795 and A. 792, *executed.*

10. *therein.* So H. 6795 and A. 792; omitted in MS and in H. 967.

11. *estate &.* H. 6795 and A. 792 omit; H. 967 follows MS.

12. *ben.* MS has comma after *ben*; H. 6795, period; A. 792, colon, which is introduced into the text.

13. *this.* No punctuation after this word in MS; H. 6795, period; A. 792, comma.

14. *His.* MS, *his.*

15. *caused.* H. 6795, *causes*; so *serves* for *served* below. A. 792 agrees with MS.

16. *pleasure.* MS has period after this word.

17. *of their.* So H. 6795 and A. 792; MS and H. 967 omit *of.*

18. *They.* MS, *they.*

19. *pallace.* So A. 792 and H. 967; H. 6795, *place.*

20. *And.* MS, *and.*

20a. Senogalia. Marginal note, hand B, *Guice hist pag: 217.*

21. *where.* So H. 6795 and A. 792; MS and H. 967 omit.

22. *benefitt and proffitt.* A. 792, *benefitt*s and *profit*s; H. 6795 omits *and proffitt*; H. 967 follows MS.

23. *alwaies.* H. 6795, *alway*; A. 792 agrees with MS.

24. *once broughte.* H. 6795 and A. 792, *brought once.*

CHAPTER IX

1. *This.* MS, *this.*

2. *see that they.* So H. 6795, A. 792; MS omits *that*; H. 967 follows MS.

3. *helpe of the Nobillitie.* In the margin, hand B, *He that comes to a principality by the helpe of the nobility shall find more adoe to preserue his authority then he that is aduanced by the people.* On the margin below, *Reasons.*

4. *obey.* MS has semicolon after *obey*; H. 6795, period.

5. *he.* So H. 6795 and A. 792; MS and H. 967, *they.*

6. *farther.* H. 6795 *further*; so below in several places.

7. *Beside.* MS, *beside.*

8. *Peoples heartes.* In the margin, hand B, *Common people mutable.*

9. *But.* MS, *but.*

10. *deceaye.* So H. 967; H. 6795, *deceyue*; A. 792 omits.

11. *rise.* H. 6795, *arise.*

12. *The.* MS, *the.*

13. *Cittizens.* So H. 967. After this word H. 6795 and A. 792 introduce *and subiectes.* This may be original, but, since the source calls for only one group (Ital., *cittadini*, Lat., *ciues*, Fr. *sujetz*), the reading of MS is allowed to stand.

Chapter X

1. *redresse.* So H. 6795 and A. 792; MS *mainteine*; H. 967, *defend.* Instead of *power* A. 792 has *force.*

2. *greate.* H. 6795, *cheefe.* In this case both A. 792 and H. 967 agree with H. 6795.

3. *other.* H. 6795, *others.*

4. *the Emperour.* H. 6795 and A. 792, *there emperour*; H. 967 follows MS.

5. *burnte.* H. 6795, *brunt*; H. 967 and A. 792 agree with MS.

6. *shootte vpp.* H. 6795 and A. 792, *pent vp*; H. 967 follows MS.

7. *these.* H. 6795 and A. 792, *those*; H. 967 follows MS.

8. *greate.* MS, no punctuation after this word; H. 6795 has period followed by capital.

9. *the prince.* So A. 792; H. 6795, *ther prince.*

10. *the seige.* H. 6795, *both before the seige & after*; A. 792 agrees with MS.

Chapter XI

1. *iurisdictions, haue.* These words are omitted in H. 6795; H. 967 and A. 792 agree with MS.

2. *the difficulties....Estates.* MS places comma after *difficulties*, no point after *gettinge*; H. 6795 omits *men*, places period after *gettinge* and writes *To*, and has *the* for *these*. H. 967, which in general follows MS, places

period after *men*; A. 792 agrees with H. 6795, but writes *provoke* for *promote*; Lat., *quem difficultates omnes priusquàm possideantur circumsistunt*; Ital. has no break in sense at this point but goes on, *perché si acquistano o per virtú o per fortuna, etc.*

3. *are of . . . themselues.* These words which appear in all other manuscripts are omitted by H. 967.

4. *principalities.* MS has semicolon after the word.

5. *onlie.* So H. 967; H. 6795 omits; A. 792, *most.*

6. *farther.* H. 6795 places colon after *farther*; MS has period and writes *for.*

7. *Yet.* MS, *yet.*

8. *there was.* So H. 967 and A. 792; H. 6795 omits.

9. *nor pettie . . . iurisdiction.* These words appear in both H. 967 and A. 792 and are yet omitted in H. 6795.

10. *soe mightie.* So H. 967 and A. 792; H. 6795, *as noble.*

11. *will not be.* So H. 967 and A. 792; H. 6795, *well to be.*

12. *revive.* H. 6795, *receave*; H. 967 and A. 792 agree with MS.

13. *The.* H. 6795, *These*; A. 792 agrees with H. 6795.

14. Columnians. H. 6795, *Calvanians*; H. 6795, *Calumons*, and MS, Calumnians for Columnians, 13 lines below.

15. *never*; H. 6795, *neyther.*

16. *must needes.* So A. 792; H. 967, *needes must*; H. 6795 omits.

17. *why.* So A. 792 and H. 967; H. 6795, *wherfore.*

18. *tooke.* H. 6795, *take*; A. 792 and H. 967 agree with MS.

19. *He.* MS, *he.*

20. *nowe.* MS, *Nowe.*

21. *by force.* So H. 967; H. 6795, *by theire force*; A. 792, *by armes.*

CHAPTER XII

1. *this matter.* So H. 967; H. 6795 and A. 792, *these matters.*

2. *many.* So A. 792; H. 6795, *remaine.*

3. *alsoe.* So H. 967; H. 6795 and A. 792 omit and write *bothe* before *to.*

4. *onlie.* H. 6795 and A. 792 omit; H. 967 follows MS.

5. *those.* So H. 967 and A. 792; H. 6795, *these.*

6. *offende or defende.* H. 6795, *defend or offend*; H. 967 and A. 792 agree with MS.

7. *The* MS, *the.*

8. *those.* H. 6795, *these*; H. 967 and A. 792 agree with MS.

9. *wantinge.* MS has period after this word; H. 6795, no point.

10. *seate.* H. 6795, *seates*; H. 967 follows MS; A. 792 has *state*, which is possibly the original reading, since Ital. has *el suo stato.*

11. *men.* MS has period after *men*; H. 6795, colon.

12. *Enemyes.* MS has comma after this word; H. 6795, colon.

13. *these mischeefes*. So H. 967; H. 6795, *this mischeife*, as also A. 792.

14. *To*. MS, *to*.

15. *there*. H. 6795, *there himself*; H. 967 and A. 792 agree with MS.

16. *streight be*. H. 6795, *be streight*; H. 967 and A. 792 agree with MS.

17. *bowndes*. So H. 967; H. 6795, *bandes*; A. 792, *bonde*.

18. *commonwealth*. So H. 967 and A. 792; H. 6795, *common weale*.

19. *hardlier*. So H. 6795 and A. 792; MS and H. 967, *hardlie*.

20. *overthrowne vtterlie*. So H. 967; H. 6795 and A. 792, *vtterly overthrowne*.

21. Macedon. H. 6795, *Macedonia*; A. 792 agrees with MS.

22. Sforza. MS places comma after Sforza; H. 6795, no punctuation.

23. *soe*. H. 6795, *for*; A. 792 and H. 967 agree with MS.

24. *thancke*. H. 6795, *thinke*; A. 792 and H. 967 agree with MS.

25. *devined*. So A. 792 and H. 967; H. 6795, *devided*.

26. *commaunded*. H. 6795, *commended*; A. 792 and H. 967 agree with MS.

27. *been*. H. 6795, *be*; A. 792 and H. 967, *bin*.

28. *looke*. So H. 967 and A. 792; H. 6795 omits.

29. *lande*. MS has no punctuation after *lande*; H. 6795 has period followed by *then*.

30. *begann.* So A. 792; H. 6795 and H. 967, *begin.*

31. *lande.* So A. 792 and H. 967; H. 6795, *bande.*

32. *the.* H. 6795 and H. 967, *theire*; A. 792, the *bondes.*

33. *had.* So H. 967; H. 6795, *held*; A. 792, *helde.*

34. *But.* MS, *but.*

35. Carmignola. MS *Caruwgola*; H. 6795 and A. 792, *Carmigola*; H. 967, *Caruivgola.*

36. *deathe.* MS places a comma after this word and writes *they.* The pointing of the text follows H. 6795.

37. *generalles.* H. 967 and H. 6795, *generall*; Lat. uses singular form; Ital., plural. The list as given in Italian is, *per loro capitani Bertolomeo da Bergamo, Ruberto da S. Severino, Conte di Pitigliano.* Petigliano. So A. 792; MS, Petiglanio.

38. *the originall.* H. 6795, *the* omitted.

39. *clergie.* H. 6795, *clergie daylye*; H. 967 follows MS; A. 792, *clergie beganne daylie.*

40. *did rise.* So H. 967; H. 6795 and A. 792, *rose.*

41. *which before ... awe.* Omitted in MS, supplied from H. 6795; H. 967 follows MS; A. 792 agrees with H. 6795; Lat., *quibus antea Imperatorum fauore oppressæ parebant*; Ital., *li quali prima favoriti dallo imperatore, le tennono oppresse.*

42. Albericus Comensis. Lat., *Alberigus Comensis;* all manuscripts have *Albericus Somensis*; Ital., *Alberigo da Conio*; Fr., *Auberi de Come.*

43. *Armies.* So A. 792; H. 6795 and H. 967, *armes.*

44. *strooke.* So H. 967; H. 6795, *stryke*; A. 792, *stroke the stroke.*

45. *an armie.* H. 6795, *one armie.*

46. *ij^m footmen.* H. 6795, *two*; A. 792, *two thousand.*

47. *they.* So A. 792; H. 6795, H. 967, *that they.*

48. *emonge.* H. 6795, *betweene*; H. 967, *amongst*; A. 792, *betwene.*

49. *They.* MS, *they.*

50. *ende.* H. 6795 places *and* after *ende;* H. 967 and A. 792 agree with MS.

CHAPTER XIII

1. *Armes.* So A. 792; H. 967 and H. 6795, *armies.*

2. *and defende.* Omitted in H. 6795; H. 967 and A. 792 agree with MS.

3. *evill.* H. 6795 and A. 792, *ill*; H. 967 follows MS.

4. *assistante.* MS has comma after this word.

5. *[not].* The negative appears in both Lat. and Ital. but in none of the English manuscripts.

6. *his.* H. 6795, *this*; H. 967 and A. 792 agree with MS.

7. *came.* Omitted in H. 6795; A. 792 agrees with MS.

8. *flight.* MS has no point after *flight.*

9. *prison.* MS, *poysen*; H. 6795 and A. 792, *prison*; H. 967, *preson*; Ital., *prigione.*

10. *theyrs.* MS places comma after *theyrs* and writes *the*; text follows H. 6795.

11. *ten tymes.* MS, *tentymes.*

12. *these.* H. 6795, *their*; H. 967 and A. 792 agree with MS.

13. *overcom.* So H. 967 and A. 792; H. 6795, *overrunne.*

14. *that.* H. 6795, *for that.*

15. Imolia *&* Furley. In other manuscripts these names are in various forms; Ital., *Imola e Furli.*

16. *neverthelesse.* MS, *Neverthelesse.*

17. *levied.* H. 6795, *loved*; H. 967 and A. 792 avoid this blunder.

18. *the kynde.* H. 6795, A. 792, and H. 967, *these kindes.*

19. Vitellians. MS has period after this word.

20. *For.* MS, *for.*

21. *armie.* The second member of the parenthesis, having been omitted by the scribe, has been inserted, probably by hand B, over a comma, after *armie.*

22. *And.* MS, *and.*

23. *thie . . . thee . . . thee*; H. 6795, *ther . . . them . . . them*; A. 792 and H. 967 agree with MS.

24. *paye.* So H. 967; H. 6795, *pension*; A. 792, *pensione.*

25. Frenche. H. 6795 and A. 792, *frenchmen.* H. 967 follows MS.

26. *lurketh.* H. 6795 has *lyeth* written over *lurketh*; H. 967 and A. 792, *lurketh.*

27. *mischeeffes*. H. 6795, *mischeife*; H. 967 and A. 792 agree with MS.

28. *owte*. H. 6795 omits; H. 967 and A. 792 agree with MS.

29. *force and strength*. So H. 967; H. 6795 and A. 792, *strengthe and force*.

30. *barbarous*. H. 6795, *barbaryans*; H. 967 and A. 792 agree with MS.

31. *prince his*. H. 6795; *prynces*, as frequently with this construction.

32. *assistantes*. MS has comma after this word and writes *but*; text follows H. 6795.

CHAPTER XIV

1. *thoughtes*. So A. 792 and H. 967; H. 6795, *thought*.

2. *to their*. H. 6795 and A. 792, *by their*; H. 967 follows MS.

3. *pleasure*. H. 6795, *pleasures*; H. 967 and A. 792 agree with MS.

4. *profession*; H. 6795, *professor*; H. 967 and A. 792 agree with MS.

5. *this*. So H. 967 and A. 792; H. 6795, *that*.

6. *soe*. H. 6795, *for*.

7. *warres*. H. 6795, *warre*; H. 967 and A. 792 agree with MS.

8. *For*. MS, *for*.

9. *practise*. On the margin, hand B, *Practise and Speculation are to be ioyned*.

10. *other.* H. 6795, *other is;* H. 967 and A. 792 agree with MS.

11. *advantage.* MS has comma after this word and writes *and;* text follows H. 6795.

12. Philopomenon. So H. 6795; MS, *Philopmenon.* In the margin, hand B, *Vide Plut. pag. 339.* The reference is evidently to Plutarch's *Life of Philopoemen* (chap. iv); no edition has been found in which page 339 contains this passage.

13. *And.* MS, *and.*

14. *histories.* In the margin, hand B, *Reading of history most necessary.*

15. *looke.* H. 6795, *take;* H. 967 and A. 792 agree with MS.

16. *councell.* H. 6795, *counselles;* so A. 792; H. 967 follows MS.

17. *fly.* H. 6795, *flee;* H. 967 and A. 792 agree with MS.

18. *conforme.* In the margin, hand B, *To apply and conforme himselfe to some person excellent.*

19. *affabilitie.* MS has no point after this word; H. 6795, a comma.

20. *ben.* Omitted in MS and A. 792; H. 6795, *bine;* H. 967, *bin.*

21. *preceptes.* H. 6795, *things* written over *preceptes.*

22. Top fol. 27r, hand B(?), *Non speciosa dictu sibi usu necessaria sequi oportet saith Curtius.*

CHAPTER XV

1. *take and.* H. 6795 and A. 792 omit; H. 967 follows MS.

2. *such.* H. 6795, *those* written over *such.*

3. *imagination.* H. 6795, *imitacion*; H. 967 and A. 792 agree with MS.

4. *lyves.* H. 6795, *lyves that* and *lyves which.* In the margin, hand B, *Shewes the Rule*: *and there is the practise of the world for which, see Cardan De Sap: 199.* The reference to Cardan would seem to be to the end of the third book of *De Sapientia,* where there is a frank discussion of the practical value of "wisdom."

5. *liker.* So H. 6795 and A. 792; MS and H. 967, *liklie.*

6. *safetie.* MS follows this word with period; H. 6795, semicolon.

7. *securitie.* MS has no punctuation after this word; H. 6795, comma.

8. *occasion.* On the margin, hand B, *Ad honesta seu prava iuxta leuis. Tac. A. 11: 33.* Tacitus writes *levi.* Below this, *humana lapidia versatili ac leui in materia* (?) *constat. Card: de Sap. he would haue hij polleticiae cuique flagitio promptus. Tac: li: 15. c: 45.* Here the writer has adapted, *ille libertus cuicumque flagitio promptus.* The apparent quotation from Cardan's *De Sapientia* is difficult to read, and the version is doubtful. No original has been found in that work.

9. *these.* H. 6795, A. 792, and H. 967, *those.*

10. *woordes.* H. 6795, *mindes*; H. 967 and A. 792 agree with MS.

11. *manie lacivious ... currishe.* This passage is omitted from H. 967. A. 792 omits *and hardie ... churlishe* and inserts *manie lowlie & gentle, manie prowde and churlish* after *chaste.*

12. *chaste.* H. 6795 places colon after *chaste.*

13. *asture.* H. 6795, *aust*ere; A. 792, *auster.*

14. *currishe.* MS places comma after this word and has no point after *behaviou*r. The pointing of the text follows H. 6795. At the bottom of fol. 26r, hand B, *In treating of Commonwealths most men set down what they should be and not what they are and vse to regulate them by their owne wills (?) education, and infused* [written over *receved?*] *opinions guided by sublimities and morallities imaginary, wherein they shew their owne capacity or hipocricy and noe more. These may be sent to vtopia, or to Platos Commonwealth.*

15. *etc.* H. 6795 and A. 792, *& so forth*; H. 967 follows MS.

16. *quallities.* MS places comma after this word and no point after *recited*; the pointing of the text follows H. 6795.

CHAPTER XVI

1. *reputed liberall.* In the margin, hand B, *To be reputed liberall of the common people a man shall vndoe himselfe and yet not please all.*

2. *handes.* MS places comma after *handes* and writes *by*; the pointing of the text follows H. 6795.

3. *neede not care greatlie.* H. 6795, *needes not greatly care*; A. 792 and H. 967 agree with MS.

4. *thrifftie or.* H. 6795 omits; A. 792 and H. 967 agree with MS.

5. *consequence.* So H. 967; H. 6795 and A. 792, *consequent.*

6. *woorthie.* So A. 792; H. 6795 and H. 967, *woorthie of.*

7. *haue ben.* So H. 967; H. 6795, *wer*; H. 967 and A. 792 agree with MS.

8. *thrifte.* So H. 6795, A. 792, and H. 967; MS, *thirste.*

9. *his charge.* So H. 967 and A. 792; H. 6795, *the charge.*

10. *shame.* H. 6795, *shonne*; H. 967, *shun*; A. 792 agrees with MS.

11. *his liberalitie.* H. 6795 omits *his*; H. 967 and A. 792 agree with MS.

12. *not be.* So H. 967 and A. 792; H. 6795, *needes be.*

13. *For.* MS, *for.*

14. *that.* So H. 967; H. 6795 and A. 792, *that which.*

15. *In.* MS, *in.*

16. *bringes.* So H. 967 and A. 792; H. 6795, *bringeth.*

CHAPTER XVII

1. *his crueltie reduced.* So H. 967 and A. 792; H. 6795, *he reduced by hys cruelty.*

2. *yt.* So H. 6795; A. 792, *it*; omitted in MS and H. 967.

3. *For.* MS, *for.*

4. *murthers and.* H. 6795, *mothers of*; H. 967 and A. 792 agree with MS.

5. *multitudes.* So H. 967; H. 6795 and A. 792, *multitude.*

6. *For.* MS, *for.*

7. *daingers.* H. 6795 and A. 792, *daunger;* H. 967 follows MS.

8. *Dido.* MS places semicolon after this word.

9. *att.* So H. 967; H. 6795 and A. 792, *for.*

10. *beloved.* So H. 967; H. 6795 and A. 792, *loved.*

11. *both.* H. 6795 omits.

12. *gayne.* After this word hand B has added *envious.*

13. *often.* H. 6795 omits; H. 967 and A. 792 agree with MS.

14. *yet in ... serve.* So H. 967; H. 6795 and A. 792, *and yet will not in tyme of neede serve.*

15. *hatredes.* So H. 967 and A. 792; H. 6795, *hatred.*

16. *For.* MS, *for.*

17. *thirst.* So A. 792 and H. 967; H. 6795, *trust.*

18. *anie.* So H. 967; H. 6795 and A. 792, *an.*

19. *reputed.* So H. 967; H. 6795 and A. 792, *termed.*

20. *either.* So H. 967 and A. 792; H. 6795 omits.

21. *his.* So H. 967; H. 6795 and A. 792, *this.*

22. *suffised.* H. 6795 and H. 967, *suffered;* A. 792 agrees with MS.

23. *lenity.* So H. 967 and A. 792; H. 6795, *levity.*

24. *obeyinge.* So H. 967 and A. 792; H. 6795, *obtainynge.*

25. *and.* So H. 967 and A. 792; H. 6795, *or,* as often.

26. *were.* So A. 792 and H. 967; H. 6795, *be.*

27. *this.* H. 6795, *Thus* preceded by period; H. 967 and A. 792 agree with MS.

28. *Kepinge.* MS, *kepinge.*

29. *or.* So A. 792; H. 6795 and H. 967, *nor.*

CHAPTER XVIII

1. *There is . . . reprehension.* It is obvious that this passage is not a translation of the Latin but of some form of the Italian. The Latin, which is abridged, is as follows: *Quàm sit omni laude dignum in principe pactum fidem seruare, atque vitę integritatem sine vllo dolo malo retinere, nemo est qui non intelligat.* The Italian is as follows: *Quanto sia laudabile in uno principe mantenere la fede e vivere con integrità e non con astuzia, ciascuno lo intende: non di manco, si vede per esperienza ne'nostri tempi quelli principi avere fatto gran cose che della fede hanno tenuto poco conto, e che hanno saputo con l'astuzia aggirare e' cervelli delli uomini; et alla fine hanno superato quelli che si sono fondati in sulla lealtà.* Gohorry's French, which follows the Italian very closely, is as follows: *Chacun entend assez qu'il est fort loüable à vn Prince de maintenir sa foy & viure en integrité nompas auecques ruses & tromperies. Neantmoins on void par experience de notre temps, que ces Princes se sont* [sic] *faits grands qui n'ont pas tenu grand conte de leur foy, & qui on sceu subtilement aueugler l'esperit des hommes lesquelz à la fin ilz on gaigné & surpassé ceux qui se sont fondez sur la loiauté.* It will be noticed that the English construction at the

beginning of the passage resembles the French rather than the Italian.

2. *faythes.* So H. 967 and A. 792; H. 6795, *faith.*

3. *who.* H. 6795, *when.*

4. *haue.* H. 6795, *hath.*

5. *kyndes . . . striffe.* So H. 967; H. 6795, *sortes of striftes or contention*; A. 792 agrees with MS, but has *dissention* for *contention.*

6. *Therefore.* MS, *therefore*; H. 6795, *Wherfore*; H. 967 and A. 792 agree with MS.

7. *woorkes.* H. 6795, *worke.* On the margin, hand B, *The antient times doe set forth in figure in that they say that Achiles and many others. Chyronis formam pulchre Alciatus magistratibus tribuit.* The reference seems to be to Emblema CXLV (*Omnia Andreæ Alciati V.C. Emblemata . . .* Per Claud. Minoem I.C. accesserunt huic editioni. Parisiis, 1618), which contains these lines:

> *Semiferum doctorem, & semiuirum Centaurum,*
> *Assideat quisquis Regibus, esse decet.*

The commentary offers an extended discussion of the particular passage of *Il Principe* against which the reference stands.

8. *bothe to imitate.* So H. 967; H. 6795, *to imitate both*; A. 792 places *both* before *of.*

9. *the* Lyon. So H. 967 and A. 792; H. 6795, *a lion.*

10. *subtile.* So H. 967 and A. 792; H. 6795, *subtility and.*

11. *to resist.* So H. 967 and A. 792; H. 6795 omits *to.*

12. *But they ... as.* These words omitted from H. 6795; H. 967 and A. 792 agree with MS.

13. *Therefore a wise ... Crafte.* The translation of this passage shows clearly that the translator was using the Latin: *Princeps propterea qui sapientia sit preditus, debet ea promissa vitare, quę suis commodis contraria fore videt. Atqui, homines si probi fuissent omnes, præceptum hoc planè fuisset inutile: verùm cum improbi sint, diligenter eorum improbitas perfidiaque erit eludenda.* The versions differ at the end, where the Italian has, *ma, perché sono tristi e non la osservarebbano a te, tu ancora non l'hai ad osservare a loro,* which is closely followed by the French.

14. *sweare.* MS, *swearve*; H. 967, *sweare*; H. 6795, *swarve*; Ital., *promettere.*

15. *naught.* So H. 967 and A. 792; H. 6795, *nought.*

16. *And.* MS, *and.*

17. *And.* MS, *and.*

18. *successe.* In the margin, hand B, *a quello che ha saputo meglio vsar la volpe e meglio successo.* This quotation from *Il Principe* is evidently translated in the text. It repeats an erroneous reading from Blado (Roma, 1532), Giolito (Vinegia, 1550), and Wolfe (London, 1584). The standard text, followed by Lat., reads *e quello che ha saputo meglio usare la volpe, è meglio capitato.* This situation may be taken as a slight indication that the translator as well as the annotator had Wolfe's edition at hand.

19. *playe the foxe.* On the margin of H. 967, *diabolus loquitur.*

20. *can.* So H. 967 and A. 792; H. 6795, *cannot.*

21. Pope Alexander. In the margin, hand B, *See Guic: pag: 4. 8.* In the 1618 edition of Fenton's translation of Guicciardini, *The Historie of Guicciardin* (London, Richard Field) censure of Pope Alexander VI occupies pages 4 and 8 and intervening pages. This may be taken as an indication of a date after which the comments in hand B were made. A further indication of date will be found in note 4, chap. xx.

22. *him.* MS has a period after *him*; H. 6795, a comma.

23. *There.* MS, *there.*

24. *with.* H. 6795, *by*, as often in this construction.

25. *were.* MS has comma after *shewe*, no point after *were.*

26. *counterfeit.* In the margin, hand B, *The credit of vertue a helpe, but* (bis) *the precise vse of it a clog and cumber to him that entends greate things saith this Atheist.*

27. *behaviour.* MS has period after this word; H. 6795, comma.

28. *soe.* H. 6795, *so loved*; A. 792, *so low*; H. 967 follows MS.

29. *religion.* MS has no point after this word; H. 6795, a colon.

30. *all.* So H. 967; H. 6795 and A. 792, *great.*

31. *did.* H. 6795, *he did.*

32. *commendacion.* H. 6795, *commendations*; H. 967 and A. 792 agree with MS.

CHAPTER XIX

1. *that.* So H. 967 and A. 792; H. 6795, *which.*

2. *contempned.* Marginal note, hand B, *Causes of contempt.*

3. *of.* H. 6795, *in.* H. 967 and A. 792 agree with MS.

4. *rockes and.* H. 6795, *rockes or;* H. 967 and A. 792 agree with MS.

5. *Maiestie.* So H. 967 and A. 792; H. 6795, *man.*

6. *and also.* H. 6795, *all also;* H. 967 and A. 792 agree with MS.

7. *they.* So H. 967 and A. 792; H. 6795, *he.*

8. *himself.* So H. 967 and A. 792; H. 6795, *him his.*

9. *subiectes.* MS. has no punctuation after *subiectes.*

10. *For.* MS, *for.*

11. *comunaltie.* So A. 792 and H. 967; H. 6795, *multitude.*

12. *For.* MS, *for.*

13. *atteyne to.* H. 6795 omits *to;* H. 967 and A. 792 agree with MS.

14. *alone.* MS has no point after *alone;* H. 6795, a comma; *they* has been altered to *he* in MS, in hand B.

15. *their.* H. 6795, *his;* A. 792 has modernized the grammar of the passage.

16. *mende.* H. 6795, *amende;* H. 967 and A. 792 agree with MS.

17. *For.* MS, *for.*

18. *either.* So H. 967; H. 6795 and A. 792, *needes.*

19. *sydes.* H. 6795, *syde;* H. 967 and A. 792 agree with MS.

20. *feare.* So A. 792 and H. 967; H. 6795, *force.*

21. *hard.* So H. 967; H. 6795 and A. 792, *sad;* H. 6795 places comma after *mistrust,* which is introduced into the text.

22. *to.* H. 6795, *as to;* H. 967 and A. 792 agree with MS.

23. *is.* H. 6795 and A. 792, *liues;* H. 967 follows MS.

24. *streyght at the.* So H. 6795; A. 792, *straight vpon;* H. 967, *strait vpon;* MS, *streyght.*

25. *non.* H. 6795, *noe,* as frequently.

26. *goodwill and common.* So H. 967; H. 6795, *common good will and;* so A. 792.

27. *discendid.* H. 6795, *discente;* A. 792, *descende.*

28. *people.* MS omits return bracket after this word.

29. *conspiracies.* Marginal note, hand B, *So long as a prince hath the hearts of the common people he neede not fear conspiracies.*

30. *he.* H. 6795, *they;* H. 967 and A. 792 agree with MS.

31. *Therefore.* MS, *therefore.*

32. *might.* MS has first member of parenthesis before *might;* H. 6795 places it before *that.*

33. *partie.* H. 6795, *partes;* A. 792, *to either parte in question.*

34. *There.* MS, *there.*

35. *principle.* Marginal note, hand B, *A wise principle.*

36. *that.* H. 6795 omits; A. 792, *so as the.*

37. *desirous therefore.* H. 6795, *therefore desirous*; H. 967 and A. 792 agree with MS.

38. *me.* MS, has period after *me*; H. 6795, comma.

39. *succeed.* So H. 967; H. 6795, *succeeded*; so also A. 792.

40. Pertinax. Written with small p, but made in a somewhat formal way; it is therefore treated here and elsewhere as a capital.

41. *the.* MS, *The.*

42. *and contrarywise.* MS shows blunder in copying. The words *and contrariwise the other imbraced a prince that was of a* are copied correctly; then follow by mistake, *gentle and courteouse disposition.* The whole passage is canceled and a new beginning made.

43. *humo*urs. MS has no point after this word; H. 6795, comma.

44. *emongst.* H. 6795, *againste*; H. 967 and A. 792 agree with MS.

45. *behavio*urs. So A. 792; H. 6795, *behaviour*; H. 967 agrees with H. 6795.

46. *to be both.* H. 6795, *both to be*; H. 967 and A. 792 agree with MS.

47. *cause.* MS has *parte to hate*; H. 6795, *partie cause to hate*, which is evidently the original reading; H. 967 and A. 792 agree with MS.

48. *goodwill.* H. 6795, *will*; H. 967 and A. 792 agree with MS.

49. *whereof.* MS, *Whereof.*

50. *those.* H. 6795, *these*; H. 967 and A. 792 agree with MS.

51. *For.* MS, *for.*

52. *commendacions.* H. 6795, *commendacion*; H. 967 and A. 792 agree with MS.

53. *manner.* H. 6795, *manners.*

54. *floorishinge.* MS, *foorishinge*; written correctly in other MSS.

55. *saide.* Return bracket omitted after this word in MS and H. 6795.

56. Iliria. H. 6795 and A. 792, *Illiria*; MS, Illicia; so also for Ilirica, five lines below; H. 967, Ilicea.

57. *goe.* H. 6795, *to goe.* After *Pertinax*, H. 6795 and A. 792 have *the emperour*; H. 967 follows MS.

58. *Empire.* H. 6795 omits parenthetical marks and writes *He.* This may be the original form.

59. *towarde.* H. 6795 and A. 792, *towardes*; H. 967 follows MS.

60. *as he . . . in* Asia. So 6795; MS, H. 967, and A. 792, *of* Asia; Ital., *volendosi insignorire di tutto lo stato*: *l'una in Asia*; Lat., *ad absolutum imperium occupandum*: *alterum in Asia.*

61. Niger. MS, niger.

62. *sending.* Hand B, bottom of fol. 35v, *Severus was a*

*right polletitian full of tricks and traynes and an ex-
quisite dissembler for his owne ends. Herodian hist.*

63. *Easterne.* H. 6795, *east*; H. 967 and A. 792 agree with
MS.

64. *favours and frendship*es. In the margin, hand B, *Merit
and seruice oblige princes but from day to day.*

65. *this.* H. 6795 and A. 792, *this greate*; H. 967 follows MS.

66. *either.* H. 6795, *ever.*

67. *he.* MS, *He.*

68. *which.* MS, *Which.*

69. *indure.* H. 6795 omits; H. 967 and A. 792 agree with MS.

70. *savage . . . vnknowen.* H. 6795, *savage & vnknowne inordinate*; A. 792, *savage, unknowen, and inordinate*;
H. 967 follows MS.

71. *of all.* H. 6795, *amonge all*; H. 967 and A. 792 agree
with MS.

72. *determination.* In the margin, hand B, *He that dispiseth
his owne life is Master of another mans.*

73. *for that.* H. 6795 and 792, *for.*

74. *iniure.* H. 6795, *inurye*; H. 967 follows MS; A. 792
agrees with H. 6795.

75. *afterwarde.* H. 6795, *afterwardes*; H. 967 and A. 792
agree with MS.

76. *succeeded.* H. 6795 omits; A. 792, *succeed*; H. 967 follows MS.

77. *and yf.* H. 6795 omits *and.*

78. *oftentymes.* H. 6795, *oftetimes*; H. 967 and A. 792 agree with MS.

79. *remaynes.* H. 6795, *remayneth*; H. 967 and A. 792 agree with MS.

80. *tyrante.* H. 6795, *tyran*; H. 967 and A. 792 agree with MS.

81. *anie.* H. 6795 omits; H. 967 and A. 792 agree with MS.

82. *For.* MS, *for.*

83. *Princes.* H. 6795, *the Princes.*

84. Turke. MS. turke.

85. *of him . . . empyre.* H. 6795 omits; H. 967 and A. 792 agree with MS.

86. Souldans. H. 6795, *soldiers*; so three lines below; H. 967, *soldiers*; A. 792, *soldians.* In the second occurrence H. 967 has *suldanes.*

87. *wynn.* H. 6795, *ioyne*; H. 967 and A. 792 agree with MS.

88. *and contempte. . . . in the.* Fols. 46 and 47 of H. 6795 are wanting.

89. *be.* So H. 967; A. 792, *shalbe.*

90. Caracalla *and* Commodus. The translation in all manuscripts omits Maximinus. Ital., *Caracalla, Commodo e Massimino*; Lat., *Caracalae, Commodo, & Maximino.*

91. *damage.* So H. 967; A. 792, *daunger.* MS corresponds to Ital., *cosa perniziosa.*

92. *imitate altogether.* So H. 967; A. 792, *altogether imitate.*

93. *for to.* A. 792, *to.*

94. *And.* MS, *and.*

CHAPTER XX

1. *Others.* MS, *others.*

2. *For.* MS, *for.*

3. *before were.* So H. 967; A. 792, *were before.*

4. *And.* MS, *and.*

5. *ancestors.* A. 792, *predecessors;* so in the line below; H. 967 follows MS; Lat. *maiores;* Ital., *li antiqui.*

6. *haue.* A. 792 omits.

7. *stryffe.* A. 792, *striffes;* H. 967, *strifes*(?).

8. *that.* Omitted in MS and in H. 967; supplied from A. 792.

9. *vnproffitable altogether.* So H. 967; A. 792, *altogether vnprofitable.*

10. *sorte.* So H. 967; A. 792, *sidde.*

11. *occasions.* So H. 967; A. 792, *reasons.* Ital., *dalle ragioni soprascritte.*

12. Guelfi. MS, Guelsi; A. 792 and H. 967 agree with MS.

13. *lampes.* MS, *Lampes.* The l is a capital in form but seems to be general for initial l.

14. Vayla. So A. 792; MS, Vayle.

15. *att grasse.* A. 792 omits, but inserts *&* before *shooke;* H. 967 follows MS.

16. *occasions.* A. 792, *occasion;* H. 967 follows MS.

17. *ladder.* So H. 967; A. 792, *lather.*

18. *in.* So. H. 967; A. 792, *for.*

19. *promise.* Beginning of fol. 48 in H. 6795.

20. *yf.* So H. 6795 and A. 792; MS, *of*; H. 967 follows MS.

21. *their.* MS, *his*; H. 6795 and A. 792, *their*; H. 967 follows MS.

22. *to.* H. 6795, *he*; H. 967 and A. 792 agree with MS.

23. *he . . . they.* MS, *they fynde that he*; H. 6795, *they fonde that he*; A. 792, *he finde that they*; H. 967, *he find that he.*

24. *alsoe feele.* So H. 967; H. 6795, *likewise finde*; A. 792, *likewise feelle.*

25. *anciente writers, & newe.* So H. 967; H. 6795 and A. 792, *ancient & new writers.*

26. *tye and.* H. 6795 omits; H. 967 and A. 792 agree with MS.

27. *the devise.* So A. 792 and H. 967; MS and H. 6795, *they devise.*

27a. *Yet.* MS, *yet.*

28. *subiection.* MS has no mark of punctuation after *subiection.*

29. Vbaldus. MS, *Voaldus*; H. 6795, *Vbald*; Lat., *Guidus Vbaldus.*

30. Valentinus. So Lat.; Ital., *Cesare Borgia.*

31. *shooved him.* Altered in MS from *shewed him self.*

32. *Yf.* MS, *yf.*

33. *once.* H. 6795 omits.

34. *holdes.* H. 6795, has *euer* after this word.

35. *of.* H. 6795 omits.

36. *coulde.* H. 6795 omits; H. 967 and A. 792 agree with MS.

CHAPTER XXI

1. *vertue.* H. 6795, *vertues*; H. 967 and A. 792 agree with MS.

2. Granada. MS, Granado.

3. *frawde though.* H. 6795, *froward thought*; H. 967 and A. 792 agree with MS; Lat., *ab innouandis rebus animu*m *auocabant*; Ital., *pensando a quella guerra, non pensavano ad innovare.*

4. *fyre.* Note at the bottom of fol. 40: *See fflorentine history p. 170 Card. 96. 488 prud: Discourses of Machiv: 599.* This chapter deals with the winning of reputation, and the references to other works by Machiavelli are easily located on the pages cited. Page 170 (seventh book near the beginning) of Bedingfield's translation, *The Florentine Historie* (London, T. C. for W. P., 1595), contains remarks about how citizens win reputation. The surprising thing is that the other reference fits a much later work, namely, Edward Dacres' translation, *Machiavels Discourses* (London, Thomas Paine for William Hills and Daniel Pakeman, 1636). Page 599 (Bk. III, chap. xxxiv) marks the beginning of a discussion of the means of acquiring popularity. This annotation cannot therefore have been written earlier than 1636. Cardan had of course plenty to say about fame, but it has not been possible to find after extended search

an edition of his works to which the annotator's references would apply.

5. *charge of his armye.* H. 6795, *church of army.*

6. *he had.* So H. 6795; MS and H. 967, *they had.*

7. *the events.* H. 6795 omits.

8. *which.* H. 6795 and A. 792 omit.

9. *his.* H. 6795 omits.

10. *administer.* H. 6795 and A. 792, *minister*; H. 967 follows MS.

11. *partie.* H. 6795, *parte.*

12. *Neither.* MS, *neither.*

13. *defended.* H. 6795, *defend*; H. 967 and A. 792 agree with MS.

14. *alwayes.* H. 6795, *alway.*

15. *syde.* MS has no point after *syde*; H. 6795, defective.

16. *shalbe.* H. 6795, *should be*; H. 967 and A. 792 agree with MS.

17. *nowe.* H. 6795 omits; H. 967 and A. 792 agree with MS.

18. *gett.* H. 6795, *take*; H. 967 and A. 792 agree with MS.

19. *losse.* H. 6795 and A. 792, *losses*; H. 967 follows MS.

20. *which all.* H. 6795 and A. 792, *that all*; H. 967 follows MS.

21. Venetians ... Frenchmen ... Millaine. These words all begin with small letters in MS.

22. *be perswaded.* H. 6795 and A. 792, *perswade himselfe;* H. 967 follows MS.

23. *tillage.* So H. 967; H. 6795, *tallage;* A. 792 omits *whether it . . . trade.*

24. *noe.* H. 6795 omits.

25. *propose.* H. 6795, *purpose;* H. 967 and A. 792 agree with MS.

26. *that.* H. 6795, A. 792, and H. 967, *and.*

27. *cause.* H. 6795, *case;* H. 967 and A. 792 agree with MS.

CHAPTER XXII

1. *in their knowledge.* H. 6795 omits; H. 967 and A. 792 agree with MS.

2. *councell.* H. 6795 and A. 792, *councellor;* Ital., *ministro.*

3. *three.* H. 6795, *these.*

4. *it self.* H. 6795 omits.

5. *An.* MS, *an.*

6. *hable.* The h in this word has been deleted by the scribe; *hable* is his usual spelling.

7. *geeven.* H. 6795, *gotten;* H. 967 and A. 792 agree with MS.

8. *last.* H. 6795, *least;* H. 967 and A. 792 agree with MS.

9. *The.* MS, *the.*

10. *and.* H. 6795, *or.*

11. *be.* H. 6795 omits; H. 967 and A. 792 agree with MS.

12. *their dutie and.* H. 6795, *the dutie and the*; H. 967 and A. 792 agree with MS.

13. *mayest.* H. 6795, *may.*

14. *the better.* H. 6795 omits; H. 967 and A. 792 agree with MS.

CHAPTER XXIII

1. *espye.* So H. 967; H. 6795, *spie*; A. 792, *spye.*

2. *avoydinge.* H. 6795, *avowinge*; H. 967 and A. 792 agree with MS.

3. *fflatterrers.* H. 6795, *flattery*; H. 967 follows MS; A. 792, agrees with H. 6795.

4. *And.* MS, *and.*

5. *into.* H. 6795, *in*; H. 967 and A. 792 agree with MS.

6. *proposed.* H. 6795, *reposed*; H. 967 and A. 792 agree with MS.

7. *boldest.* So A. 792 and H. 967; H. 6795, *boldliest.*

8. *contrariety.* H. 6795, *contrarieties*; H. 967 and A. 792 agree with MS.

9. *quicklie.* H. 6795, *greatly*; H. 967 and A. 792 agree with MS.

10. *talkinge.* H. 6795, *talkinge once*; H. 967 and A. 792 agree with MS.

11. *desyred.* MS has period after *desyred.*

12. *to noe.* H. 6795 and A. 792, *with noe*; H. 967 follows MS.

13. *this.* H. 6795, *these.*

14. *one.* H. 6795 and A. 792, *in one.*

15. *the next.* H. 6795 and A. 792, *in the next*; H. 967 follows MS.

16. *bylde anie certeintie.* H. 6795, *blind any certen eie.* H. 967 and A. 792 agree with MS.

17. *lyke.* H. 6795 and A. 792, *list*; H. 967 follows MS.

18. *by.* H. 6795, *but.*

19. *devise.* H. 6795 and A. 792, *advise*; H. 967 follows MS.

20. *it may.* H. 6795, *may it*; H. 967 follows MS; A. 792 confuses the passage by writing, as often, *yet* for *it.*

21. *his.* H. 6795, *this*; H. 967 and A. 792 agree with MS.

22. *as they.* So A. 792 and H. 967; H. 6795, *of ther.*

23. *proane.* H. 6795, *prove*; H. 967 and A. 792 agree with MS.

CHAPTER XXIV

1. *but.* Canceled in H. 6795; H. 967 and A. 792 agree with MS.

2. *the estate.* H. 6795 and A. 792, *his estate*; H. 967 follows MS.

3. *their parentes.* H. 6795, *the princes*; H. 967 and A. 792 agree with MS.

4. *lynes.* H. 6795, *lives*; H. 967 and A. 792 agree with MS; Ital., *il sangue antico*; Lat., *ipsa stirpis antiquitas.*

5. *these.* H. 6795 and A. 792, *those*; H. 967 follows MS.

6. *providing.* So A. 792 and H. 967; H. 6795, *proceedinge.*

7. *States.* H. 6795, *seates*; H. 967 and A. 792 agree with MS.

8. *bownde*s. H. 6795, *ban*[*des*]; A. 792, *bondes*; H. 967, *bounde*s.

9. *thoughe.* So H. 967 and A. 792; H. 6795, *althoughe.*

10. *their.* So H. 967 and A. 792; H. 6795, *their owne.*

11. *For.* MS, *for.*

12. *weried.* H. 6795, *wearie*; H. 967 and A. 792 agree with MS.

13. *hope.* MS has a period after *hope*; H. 6795, a comma.

14. *fall.* MS has comma after *fall. in.* H. 6795, *into.*

15. *For that.* MS has *for that.*

16. *chaunces.* H. 967, A. 792, and H. 6795, *chaunceth.*

17. *causes.* So H. 967; H. 6795 and A. 792, *cases.*

18. *or yf.* So H. 6795; MS *for yf*; A. 792 agrees with H. 6795; H. 967 follows MS; Lat., *aut si sit.*

19. *live.* H. 6795 omits *live* and inserts *be* after *continewally.*

20. *For.* MS, *for.*

CHAPTER XXV

1. *such sort . . . by.* Not in MS; added from H. 6795, where the omitted words occupy exactly one line. This fact, however, since the chapter is just beginning and both are folio manuscripts, need not indicate that MS is

copying from H. 6795. A. 792 agrees with H. 6795. H. 967 with MS.

2. *to.* H. 6795 omits; H. 967 and A. 792 agree with MS.

3. *And.* MS, *and.*

4. *seen.* H. 6795 omits.

5. *Fortune.* In the margin, hand B, *his opinion of fortune.*

6. *of earth.* H. 6795, *or darth*; H. 967 and A. 792 agree with MS.

7. *overflowe.* H. 6795, *over flowes*; H. 967 and A. 792 agree with MS.

8. *her.* MS has period after *her*; H. 6795, comma.

9. *as.* H. 6795 and A. 792, *for*; H. 967 follows MS.

10. *surely.* H. 6795 omits; A. 792, *securely*; H. 967 follows MS.

11. *the one.* So H. 6795; MS, *that one.*

12. *discreation.* H. 6795 and A. 792 add *and moderacion*, which may be original, since one finds in the Italian *con respetti e pazienza*; but the translation is so far from the original in this passage that it is not possible to say definitely.

13. *states.* H. 6795 and A. 792, *state*; H. 967 follows MS.

14. *councelles.* In the margin, hand B, *two men gaine one and the same thing by diuerse counsells.*

15. *other twoe.* H. 6795 and A. 792, *other twoe men*; H. 967 follows MS.

16. *crosse.* So H. 967; H. 6795, *thwarde*; A. 792, *thwarte.*

17. *devises.* H. 6795, *device*; in MS *devises* has been deleted and *proceeding* added in the margin in hand B.

18. Pope Iulius. At this point in H. 364 a second hand begins, but the version does not agree with version A until the beginning of chapter xxvi.

19. *state.* H. 6795, *states*; H. 967 and A. 792 agree with MS.

20. *evill.* H. 6795 and A. 792, *ill.*

21. *quandarie.* Marginal note, hand B, *tis good keeping an enemy between feare and hope.*

22. *For.* MS, *for.*

23. *with.* H. 6795, *which.*

24. *daynted.* All other manuscripts have *daunted.*

25. *hym.* This word in MS seems to be a correction of *them*; H. 967 has *them*; H. 6795 and A. 792, *him.*

26. *For.* MS, *for.*

27. *rule.* H. 6795 places colon after *rule.*

CHAPTER XXVI.

1. From this point the version presented in H. 364 is the same as that of MS, H. 6795, A. 792, and H. 967.

2. *specified.* H. 364, H. 967, and A. 792 all place a comma after *specified.* The punctuation of these manuscripts is usually fuller and more modern than that of MS and H. 6795.

3. *honor.* So 6795 and A. 792; MS, H. 364, and H. 967 omit this necessary word.

4. *sorte.* So H. 967; H. 364, *sortes.*

5. *Iudgmente.* MS has period after this word.

6. *by.* MS shows *for* canceled, with *by* written above it, in hand B; H. 6795, A. 792, and H. 364 have *by*; H. 967 has *for.*

7. *state.* So H. 6795 and H. 967; H. 364, *estate.* The form of the word varies in the manuscripts throughout.

8. *standes.* H. 6795, *nowe stands*; H. 967, A. 792, and H. 364 agree with MS.

9. *lived and floorished.* So H. 6795, A. 792, and H. 967; H. 364, *flourished, & lived.*

10. *coorrage.* MS has period after this word.

11. *of.* H. 364 omits, places a period after *destitute*, and writes *God*, thus confusing the text. Other manuscripts agree with MS.

12. *guyde or aucthor.* So A. 792, which is evidently the original reading; Lat., *ducem, authoremque*; MS, followed by H. 967, *aucthor*; H. 6795, *or aucthor.* The word *guyde* has been omitted from H. 6795, which thus occupies a transitional position between the original and MS.

13. *soveraigne Principalitie.* In the margin, hand B, *Leo x^{th} pope at that tyme.*

14. *neither.* H. 6795, *neuer*; A. 792, H. 967, and H. 364 agree with MS.

15. *that waye . . . them.* Translation of a passage inaccurately cited by Machiavelli from Livy, IX, 1: *iustum enim est bellum quibus necessarium, et pia arma ubi nisi in armis spes est.* Lat. takes this over in the following

form: *Nam id bellum est iustum, quod est necessarium: & ea arma pietatem redolent, cum nulla alia in re, quàm in illis spes omnis vertitur.* This was either misunderstood by the English translator or the version has been variously corrupted. The text restores the probable original. It is possible that *in them* became *in him* and that this caused some copyist of the manuscript to write *generalles hope* (as in MS; H. 6795, *generalls hope*); A. 792 has, correctly, *generall hope* (*spes omnis*).

16. *meane.* So H. 6795 and H. 967; H. 364, *meanes.*

17. *for.* H. 6795 and H. 967, *of*; H. 364, *for.*

18. *rocke.* The Blado text and the Giolito text read *pieta* for *pietra,* and thus make nonsense of the passage. Telius, based on the second Aldine text, which in this passage followed Blado, reads *pietas aquam effudit.* Wolfe corrects this error. This passage, therefore, offers a slight indication that our translator had Wolfe's edition by him. On this passage see Orsini, *Studii sul Rinascimento italiano in Inghilterra,* pp. 16-17.

19. *concurr.* So A. 792, H. 967 and H. 364; H. 6795, *incurre.*

20. *God.* MS, *god.*

21. *the woonted.* H. 364 has *they wanted,* one of a good many peculiarities of that manuscript, which are not noted unless they affect some other version.

22. *extinguished.* H. 6795 and A. 792 add after this word *& quencht*; Ital., *spenta*; Lat., *extincta*; H. 967 and H. 364 follow MS.

23. *synce.* H. 6795, *such*; A. 792, H. 967, and H. 364 agree with MS.

24. *will.* So H. 967 and H. 364; H. 6795 and A. 792, *shall.*

25. *that.* MS places a comma after *that.*

26. *thincketh.* So H. 967 and H. 364; H. 6795, *thinkes.*

27. Alexandria. MS has no punctuation mark after this word, which, however, stands at the end of a line. In such cases punctuation is often lacking in MS.

28. *intende.* H. 6795, *intent*; H. 967 and H. 364 follow MS.

29. *examples.* So H. 967; H. 6795, *example*; so H. 364.

30. *thy.* H. 967, *thine*; H. 6795 and H. 364, *their.*

31. *And therefore.* At this point H. 6795 and H. 364 agree in showing no paragraph; H. 967 follows MS.

32. *every respecte.* So H. 967 and H. 364; H. 6795, *all respect*es.

33. *to.* H. 6795, *vnto*; A. 792, H. 364, and H. 967 agree with MS.

34. *And this.* In this case H. 6795 shows no paragraph and H. 364 and H. 967 agree with MS.

35. *expresse.* H. 6795 and A. 792 add *in word*es; H. 364 and H. 967 agree with MS.

36. That valiante ... heartes. H. 6795 writes this verse as prose; so also does A. 792. The only variation in text in H. 6795 is *from* for For in the third line; A. 792 has *for*. H. 967 has *gainst* for againste. H. 364 has *barbarians* for barbarous.

On a blank leaf at the end of the manuscript hand B has written as follows:

This booke not only discovers the knowledge of much euill, but also the shortest and most effectuall waies to perpetrate the same. Here is shewed that we should not with a rude heate or naturall instinct or by other example but artificially as it were only for a further end follow ether vertue or vice, making noe difference but by the profit we may receiue when we haue occasion to vse them. the Author teacheth what men doe and not what they ought to doe. this Machivele expresseth of himselfe in the 5th of his Fflorentine history where he thus writeth SS in declaring things hapned in this bad world, we shall not set downe the vertue of any Captaine the Courage of any Souldier or the loue of any Citicen towards his Country yet you shall see what cunning aid all(?) princes and great men haue vsed to mayntayne the reputation they did not deserve which will perchance prooue no lesse worthy to be knowen then those of antient tyme and albeite the actions of our moderne princes are not to be admired for their vertue and greatnes yet for other qualities they are with noe lesse admiration considered seeing so many noble mynds were by so few and corrupt kept vnder and in awe.

The words *or by other example* have been crowded in at the end of the line and in the margin. Above the word *difference* is written what looks like *of rule*. After *writeth* there are two roughly made letters, possibly SS for (sequentiae?). The words *princes and great men* have been written over another word, possibly *governers*. On the bottom of the sheet are scribbles, probably in hand B, *pag. 4. 16. 27* and *pag. 29.*